CRICC

SURJIT S. BHALLA is chairman of Oxus Investments, a portfolio management and emerging markets advisory firm. He has worked as a research economist at the Rand Corporation, Brookings Institution, World Bank and The Policy Group. In addition, he has worked in asset management at the World Bank, Goldman Sachs, and Deutsche Bank. His first book, *Between the Wickets: The Who and Why of the Best in Cricket*, developed a model for evaluating performance in cricket.

ANKUR CHOUDHARY is an investment consultant and the co-founder of AlphaFront.com—an online investment advisory start-up. He has worked as a quantitative analyst in the financial markets for several years, with his last stint being at a leading global hedge fund in 2014. He holds a Bachelors degree in Computer Science from IIT, Kanpur.

Praise for the Book

'Who would win, West Indies or Australia, on a sticky pitch, with an injured strike bowler—even across the ages? Surjit S. Bhalla and Ankur Choudhary provide answers in *Criconomics*, a pioneering and gloriously intriguing attempt to understand the game through statistical modelling. It has the potential to change how cricket is discussed, judged, coached and played.'

—James Astill, Political Editor of *The Economist* and author of *The Great Tamasha*

'More than a quarter of a century ago, I chaired one of the most remarkable seminars ever to take place at the London School of Economics. It was the launch of *Between the Wickets* by Surjit S. Bhalla, the first systematic statistical (indeed "econometric") analysis of the entire Wisden data for Test cricket. We realized for the first time, with any sort of rigour, how to understand the questions, who was the best captain, the best team, which were the most docile wickets etc. It was the ultimate reference for argumentative cricket fans, sports buffs and statistical nerds. And it was the predecessor and foundation for all the flashes and numbers that now appear on your screens whilst watching cricket.

Criconomics now does this for the one-day game with the same sense of curiosity, contrariness, sensible and wacky questions, and enjoyment of life and sport. A fascinating contribution and a testimony to the observation that sport, life, statistics and obsession can be great fun.'

—Lord Nicholas Stern, IG Patel Professor of Economic and Government at LSE, and President of the British Academy

CRICONOMICS

*Everything You Wanted to Know
About ODI Cricket
and More*

Surjit S. Bhalla

Ankur Choudhary

RUPA

First Published by
Rupa Publications India Pvt. Ltd 2015
7/16, Ansari Road, Daryaganj
New Delhi 110002

Sales centres:
Allahabad Bengaluru Chennai
Hyderabad Jaipur Kathmandu
Kolkata Mumbai

ISBN: 978-81-291-3577-3

First impression 2015

10 9 8 7 6 5 4 3 2 1

To my parents, Sushila and Bijay Kr. Choudhary

—Ankur

To the memory of the schoolboys of Peshawar's Army Public School and College, and young Phil Hughes, whose lives were cut short this year: yours was the earth and everything that was in it. You will not be forgotten.

CONTENTS

PREFACE

People say that analysis of cricket, or any other sport, takes away the beauty of the game. A few months ago, I would have conceded and nodded in agreement, in a sheepishly guilty way. Writing this book has changed that. Numbers have, in fact, introduced me to the beauty of this game and its players. I must confess that I haven't watched a lot of cricket. Throughout my teenage and young adulthood years, the only World Cup India had won was in 1983—two years before I was born. Yet, I had never felt the urge to watch any of its footage.

But, one night while working on the chapter of World Cup upsets, after I had just finished discussing how India were the underdogs in the finals, I suddenly found myself on YouTube looking for a video of the match. I found an hour-long video and even though I was quite sleepy, I watched the entire footage—most of it in low resolution. When Kapil Dev was running backwards looking over his shoulders for the Viv Richards catch, I held my breath and caught myself thinking, for a split second—will he make it? It is not as though I didn't know what would happen. Of course, he would take the catch and yes, we were the weaker team. I might have even seen a clip of the catch on TV before but in any case, it had never registered.

But this time it was different. Because now I knew Richards. Now I knew the West Indies of that decade. Now I could imagine what the Indian team must have felt after winning that match. Today when I look at that photograph of Kapil Dev holding the Cup, it evokes a warm fuzzy feeling.

When I thought I was crunching numbers, I was actually travelling through time, witnessing each match through the eyes of our model. There were upsets, there were comebacks, heroes were born—some burnt out, some faded away and a few, the world was sorry to let go. There is beauty in numbers too.

Ankur Choudhary

My experience with cricket could not be more different from Ankur's. Most likely, it is the age gap. I was born in 1948, much before the age of television, let alone the distractions of the internet. Urbanization was still many years away, and there were lots of open spaces for makeshift turning pitches! So, I lived and breathed and played cricket in my schoolboy youth. Watching Test cricket was indirect. If one wanted to see cricket in action, one had to go and watch films. All films were preceded by a newsreel, and the newsreel contained snippets of the latest Test match. Hence, the twin birth of my two major passions—cricket and films. Oh yes, and numbers too.

As a player, I preferred to bat as an opener. I can't actually remember ever wanting to be a bowler. But I have to admit more than a shade of envy in watching bowlers—either good pace or good leg-spin. Try as I might, I could never flip my wrists; and never could bowl fast—hell, not even medium. Perhaps that is why I enjoy watching a good pace bowler—or a Shane Warne.

I lost my connection with active cricket when in 1965 I

went to attend Purdue University in West Lafayette, Indiana—middle of mid-America, and not exactly a home of cricket. However, I kept up with all the cricket in the world with a daily trudge to the library to read a three-day-old *London Times*. And just to not lose my grip on the game, I 'batted' in my class by demonstrating (with my Indian bat), the 'equivalence' between baseball and cricket. Life got better in 1969 when I moved to Silicon Valley to work as a software engineer. There was a Northern California cricket league in which I played, and I was home again.

Fast forward to the early 1980s—the world was fast changing and I could now jointly indulge in two of my three obsessions—numbers and cricket. The indulgence was straightforward. The Kalman filter used to estimate currency and bond trading algorithms could now be used to estimate batting and bowling strength of teams. Thus, in 1987 I wrote my first book on cricket. Now, thirty years later, I am joined by an ace computer programmer. I know more about cricket—he knows more about programming!

Surjit S. Bhalla

We have enjoyed this journey—a quixotic quest. We hope you do the same. If you do, write to us at our website *www.criconomics.com* and let us know. If you don't...well, let us know anyway. Enjoy.

LIST OF TABLES

LIST OF BOXES

LIST OF FIGURES

DATA NOTE

All CricketX analysis presented in the book is based on ODI (One Day International) matches played between the ten full-members of ICC (International Cricket Council) mentioned below. Matches which were interrupted by rain, poor light, etc and were decided by the Duckworth-Lewis method have been excluded from the calculations.

The Ten Full Members of ICC:

1. AUS—Australia
2. ENG—England
3. IND—India
4. SL—Sri Lanka
5. NZ—New Zealand
6. PAK—Pakistan
7. SA—South Africa
8. WI—West Indies
9. ZIM—Zimbabwe
10. BAN—Bangladesh

DATA SOURCES

One of the two authors, Surjit S. Bhalla, published a book on Test cricket in 1987, called *Between the Wickets: The Who and Why of the Best in Cricket*. For it, he along with colleagues K. Seetharaman and Vikesh Sethi, built, for the *first time ever*, a computerized database of score cards of all Test matches till then using Bill Frindall's *The Wisden Book of Test Cricket, 1877–1984*. In the mid-1990s, Surjit Bhalla and Itu Chaudhuri developed CricketX and kept updating their computerized database of Test and ODI matches till about 2001, when they supplied it to Cricinfo. The data of matches since then has been obtained from the Cricinfo website.

1

THE QUEST

We shall not cease from exploration
And the end of all our exploring
Will be to arrive where we started
And know the place for the first time.

~T.S. Eliot, *Little Gidding*

The times are not changing, they have already changed. Debate, unfortunately, has lost much of its fervour as we instantly turn to our smartphones to check the facts during an argument. When did Bob Dylan sing 'Like a Rolling Stone'? Who was the director of *Gone With the Wind*? All the information we need is now available at our fingertips.

How much do you know about cricket? Do you know who is the greatest batsman in cricket history? You don't need to check online for what is common knowledge—Don Bradman. Even if many of us did not live to see Don Bradman bat, countless reports from those who did, and more importantly his statistics, clearly bear out the fact that he was the greatest batsman who ever lived. Indeed, we would venture to say that if an analysis of sportspersons is done, Bradman is likely to emerge as the greatest athlete ever. To be sure, Bradman will have competition from the likes of Jesse Owens, the American sprinter-athlete who thumbed his, and the world's, nose at Adolf Hitler in the 1936 Olympics. Owens won the gold medal in four events during the Olympics—the 100 metre and 200 metre dash, the 400 metre run, and the long jump. His (then) world record for 100 metre—10.2 seconds—remained unbroken for twenty years. Owens' long jump record was only broken some fifty years later by another American athlete—Carl Lewis.

There will also be competition for the greatest athlete prize from Muhammad Ali, Rod Laver, Roger Federer, Babe Ruth, Michael Jordan, Tiger Woods, Steffi Graf and others. Apologies to the greatest sportsmen, and sportswomen, not mentioned, but you get the point, and the purpose of our endeavour. You will not be able to get an answer to the question of the greatest athlete, or the question of who is the greatest one-day cricket batsman, bowler, or team, from Siri or the internet.

But can we? And if yes, how will our answers be different from those of cricket commentators and fans? Well, being economists, we have done it with *models*, i.e. we have constructed an analytical framework called CricketX, that models the game of cricket and the various stages through which it progresses, from the first over to the last. This means that our claims are *not* based on our subjective opinions about the game; instead, they follow from the model that we have constructed and hence are backed by statistical rigour. In this book, we share our framework and use it to answer some of the most interesting questions about One Day International (ODI) cricket. We extend the first such effort made nearly thirty years ago in *Between the Wickets: The Who and Why of the Best in Cricket* (hereafter referred to as BTW).

BTW analysed the 110-year history of Test cricket—from 1877 to 1987. Yes, it did confirm that Don Bradman was the greatest batsman. It did not answer the other important question of the greatest athlete, and neither does this book. That is left for a third book.

Since this book is about analysis, and forecasts, our credibility is enhanced by this forecast that was made in 1987, contained in page 5 of BTW: *'And in this age, it is mandatory to think of a sequel. So if you have bought this book, you have implicitly registered a demand for financing the inevitable—a sequel on one-day cricket.'*

The Journey Begins...

Cricket, like baseball, is blessed with numbers and statistics. When BTW was written in the mid-1980s, computers were a luxury. The personal computer (PC) had made its appearance some six years before, in 1981. Then came the laptop, the notebook, the tablet... Computation is no longer a problem. But in-depth analysis is still relatively scarce, and knowledge scarcer. Hence, it is our ambition to unearth new cricketing knowledge by conducting rigorous research, even if it flies in the face of conventional wisdom. And a beginning has been made. In this book, we provide new and better ways to analyse cricket teams and players, with one-day cricket as our prism. Towards this end, we also make prescriptions for the future of

Test cricket and T20 cricket based on the insights generated by our models. But that is getting ahead of the story.

One other politically correct concern. We were schoolboys when we played cricket, and hence our mention of what schoolboys think, and do. But along with the computer, the world is a lot different, and better, today than it was thirty years ago. There are schoolgirls who play cricket, and since we are all agog about double centuries in one-day cricket, it is most important to acknowledge that Belinda Clark of Australia was the first *cricketer* to score a double century in this format of the game. So we take a bow as do Virender Sehwag, Sachin Tendulkar and Rohit Sharma. Cricket, like many other sports, is now a universal game. So while we refer to him rather than her, schoolboy rather than schoolgirl, we mean no bias.

Talking about double centuries in cricket, what does it show about the game that the three male double centuries in ODI cricket were all scored in India and by Indians? That Indian pitches are the most batsman friendly in the world. Prior to the late 1980s, India had the 'Killing Fields' of Test cricket—match after match was drawn, on pitches meant to destroy the sport by draining it of all competition. There is some chance of the same happening in ODI cricket today; lessons to be learnt from history.

Sir Bradman's letter on receipt of the book *Between the Wickets: The Who and Why of the Best in Cricket*.

Adelaide
18/12/87

Dear Doctor Bhalla,

Thank you for your letter and your kindness in sending me a copy of your book. It produces most interesting reading.

I don't profess to understand computer technique and it is beyond me how a computer can recognise such an abstract thing as "quality", as distinct from pure mathematics. Also how can a computer "think".

It can only produce answers to what is fed into it.

Having said that, let me say that there is so little between leading batsmen over history that anyone could produce say a rational best 10.

Bowlers are much more difficult & I must be honest & say my bowling findings would be very different from the computer rankings.

In my radio talks due to start on Dec 30 & continue weekly for 2 months I have towards the end proven my ideas on great players. If you are able to listen you'd be interested. We are not that far apart.

Best wishes for Xmas and 1988.

Yours sincerely,

Don Bradman

Following is a transcript of Sir Bradman's letter. Note that in his last praragraph, Sir Bradman comments on the similarity of his and Surjit's ranking.

Adelaide
18/12/1987

Dear Doctor Bhalla,

Thank you for your letter and your kindness in lending me a copy of your book.

It produces most interesting reading.

I don't profess to understand computer technique and it is beyond me how a computer can recognize such an abstract thing as "quality", as distinct from pure mathematics. Also how can a computer "think". It can only produce answers to what is fed into it.

Having said that, let me say that there is so little between leading batsmen over history that anyone could produce say a rational best 10.

Bowlers are much more difficult—I must be honest and say my bowling findings would be different from the computer rankings.

In my radio talks due to start on Dec. 26 and continue weekly for 2 months, I have towards the end given my ideas on great players. If you are able to listen, you'd be interested. We are not that far apart.

Best Wishes for Xmas and 1988.

Yours sincerely,
Don Bradman

Analysis of a pitch and how it impacts performance is just part of our story. What we attempt in this book is an analysis of all facets of performance in cricket—the batsman, the bowler and the team. We start with the observation that a cricket match is a simple contest between a bat and a ball. The bowler hurls the ball, and the batsman hits it and scores runs. If it was just a two-person event like tennis, the job would have been simpler, but cricket is a team sport. And there are two distinct acts involved—batting and bowling (this includes fielding). How do you assess team strength while accounting for quality of opposition? And then, how do you isolate the performance of individual players from that of the team? And even if that were possible, how do you now compare their different attributes (strike rate v batting average, economy v bowling average) and rank them? You get the drift. This book provides an answer to these, and many other questions.

One issue in particular stands out—forecasting of match results. There is an inherent curiosity in human nature—we want to know about an event before it happens. For example, we spend so much time, effort and energy in forecasting the results of an election. One can understand speculating about the outcome of an election and analysing who will win months in advance. But an exit poll about the results that will be revealed in a few days' time? Or projecting a winner hours before the result is out? One reason for the excitement is there is money to be made. Another reason is the human need for prediction and control, even if it is superficial, which underlies most, if not all, human endeavours—from religion to science.

It is difficult to imagine sport today without prediction. Forget today—history is replete with examples of bets being made, e.g. which scorpion would win a race, or which gladiator would triumph against a lion. Prediction is a necessary concomitant of any sport, and the gentleman's sport of cricket is no exception. Apart from just satisfying some primal needs of us humans, prediction is necessary to measure the validity of knowledge. It is, along with observation, the foundation of the scientific process. The worth of a theory or any model lies solely in the accuracy of the predictions it makes. As a corollary, a model which cannot make any predictions is useless.

It is prediction which makes our analysis on ODI cricket different from most others. We subject our model, our analysis, to a trial by fire based on its precision in predicting the future. If it can predict the outcomes to a *reasonable* extent, it is a good model and its findings can be taken more seriously than those of others which do not allow for prediction or its measurement. We discard what is not predictive even if it conforms to received wisdom and we accept what is predictive, even though it might come as a surprise to us. There are no holy cows. The authenticity of all our assessments of players, and teams—their brilliance, their greatness—stems from this ability to predict.

We unveil our analytical model on ODI cricket in the remaining nine chapters of this book. Chapter 2 outlines our framework and brings forth the conceptual (and real!) issues involved in assessing the best and the greatest. Chapters 3 to 7 evaluate, describe and list the greatest teams, batsmen, bowlers, all-rounders and captains in ODI cricket. Chapter 8 is an attempt to answer a slightly different question—who plays best under stress and tension? We have all speculated on this phenomenon, and we present an initial analytical stab at this great unknown. Chapter 9 makes a bold attempt at forecasting the winner of the eleventh cricket World Cup to be played in Australia and New Zealand, in February–March 2015. Chapter 10 does not conclude but, instead, recommends strategic changes required in the game of Test cricket, T20 and ODI cricket.

2

WHAT'S IT ALL ABOUT?

2A. A Brief History of ODI Cricket

If I knew that I was going to die today,
I think I should still want to hear the cricket scores.

~G.H. Hardy

Cricket and baseball are two sports that traditionally have had a lot of information available about them. We say traditionally because today every sport has a multitude of numbers describing the course of a game, and the performances of players.

Before the age of computing, a cricket fan was judged by his memory for cricket statistics, and his ability to reproduce them at will. A boy quoting verses from Shakespeare's *Julius Caesar*, or from T.S. Eliot's *The Wasteland*, was not as interesting as someone who could recount the last moments of the incredible tied Test between Australia and West Indies in mid-December 1960. (I [Surjit] remember that vividly because the match happened in the middle of my seventh grade final exams—the joys of short-wave radio.) Or recall, with deadly accuracy, the brilliance of Sunil Gavaskar's 774 runs in West Indies in his debut series in 1971.

Cricket has its glorious uncertainties—and at its core, this book is about resolving some of them. Put simply, the puzzle we are attempting to solve is how does cricket work. It is also about predicting the broad contours of a match from the information available *before* the match takes place. Of course, no attempt is made to predict a tied Test (though the chances of getting a tie prediction right in ODIs is considerably higher—out of 3,552 matches played since the inception of ODIs in 1971, thirty-two have been tied versus only two in Test cricket out of 2,146 played since 1871!)

Box 2A.1: Who Said Five Is the Limit? Timeless Tests

'A timeless Test is a match of Test cricket played under no limitation of time, which means the match is played until one side wins or the match is tied, with theoretically no possibility of a draw' (Wikipedia). All Tests played in Australia (including Ashes) from 1883 to 1937 were timeless matches played to a finish. Outside Australia, there were only a handful of such matches. The last ever and the longest timeless Test was the fifth Test between England and South Africa at Durban in 1939, which was mutually agreed to be a draw after nine days of play, otherwise the England team would have missed the boat for home.

Background

The first international one-day match was played in Melbourne on 5 January 1971, between Australia and England. It was so early in the season that it was adjudged as the first ODI ex-post. In those days, this format was called LOI, which stood for Limited Overs International. Also, in those days, the number one song was 'Joy to the World' by Three Dog Night, and Australian matches were played as eight-ball overs. The ODI in Melbourne was a forty overs match—equivalent to a 53.2 six-ball overs match. The first *official* ODI was played some twenty months later in England in August 1972 and it was a fifty-five overs match. Later on, as experiments continued, there were sixty overs matches—indeed India's World Cup victory in 1983 was one such. Soon after, the world converged to a fifty overs match format, not far from the original intention.

ODI Cricket—From a Gentleman's Game to a Batsman's Game

Like any other sport, ODI cricket has also undergone several changes over time—from a game once played in white flannels on sunny days with a cherry-red ball to colourfully attired players sweating it out under floodlights. The game now uses a complicated statistical algorithm, the Duckworth-Lewis method, to guide its outcome in case the rain gods decide to have some fun at our expense. The game has also evolved because of the spirit of innovation from its players and organizers. (Box 2A.2 presents a timeline of the history of ODI cricket and the major changes it has undergone.)

However, all the changes have not been for the better. Table 2A.1 documents how ODI cricket scores have evolved over the four-and-a-half decades since the first match. The steady upward trajectory of Runs Per Over (RPO) is unmistakable.

Table 2A.1: Evolution of ODI Cricket

Decade	Average First Innings				
	Score	Wickets	Overs	RPO	RPW
1970s	202	8	48	4.2	29
1980s	210	7	47	4.5	32
1990s	223	8	48	4.6	34
2000s	234	8	47	4.9	35
2010s	241	8	47	5.1	35
Average	228	8	47	4.8	34

Source: CricketX database

There have been two main reasons for this uptrend—fielding restrictions and technology. Wikipedia offers a concise history of the fielding restrictions:

> Fielding restrictions were first introduced in 1992, with only *two* fieldsmen allowed outside the circle in the first fifteen overs, then five fieldsmen allowed outside the circle for the remaining overs. This was shortened to ten overs in 2005, and two five-over powerplays were introduced, with the bowling team having discretion over the timing for both. In 2008, the batting team was given discretion for the timing of one of the two powerplays.... Finally, in 2012, the bowling powerplay was abandoned, and the number of fielders allowed outside the 30-yard circle during *non-powerplay* overs was reduced from *five to four*. (emphasis added)

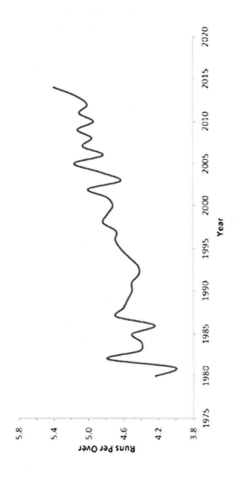

A Batsman's Game: Runs Per Over in First Innings Over Time

Fielding restrictions including the recently introduced powerplays, better bats and flatter pitches have steadily tilted the game towards batting, evident in the upward trajectory of RPO.

So while before 1992 we had five fielders outside the 30-yard circle, for all fifty overs, giving us a total of 250 fielder-overs at the boundaries, today we have two fielders outside the circle in the first ten overs, three during the batting powerplay of five overs and four otherwise. That's only 175 fielder-overs at the ropes, a full 30 per cent reduction in fielding 'strength', if you will. This alone is enough to tilt the balance in favour of batsmen. But there is more.

While better fitness of players has benefited both sides, improvements in technology have come to the aid of the batsmen more than the bowlers. Niranjan Rajadhyaksha, executive editor of the business daily *Mint*, recently commented:

> It is a common grouse that batsmen have benefited from better bats. Even a mis-hit soars above the boundary these days. Tennis players also have better rackets, but the competitors on both sides of the net have equal access to the tools of power tennis. In cricket, on the other hand, contests have become imbalanced because bowlers have had no comparable technological advance to take advantage of. Even some cricket balls are made to swing less these days.

There is one final deal-sweetener for the batsmen—the pitch. Pitches today are being made flatter, and more batsmen friendly, and nowhere is this truer than in India. The culmination of all these distortions is evident in the 264-run knock by Rohit Sharma against Sri Lanka on 13 November 2014, in Kolkata.

Is it then any surprise that the innovations from the perennially disadvantaged bowlers—the *doosra* and the reverse swing—are so much more lethal (and shrouded in controversy) than those by the prodigal batsmen—the reverse sweep, switch hit and the helicopter shot?

Box 2A.2: Timeline: A Brief History of ODI Cricket

Reverse sweep and reverse swing invented by Pakistan in 1970s	**1971**	First ODI: Australia v England at Melbourne
First World Cup: West Indies beat Australia in final at Lord's	**1975**	
	1976	First women's match at Lord's, England v Australia
	1980	6-ball overs become standard
India wins the World Cup	**1983**	
First 50 overs World Cup	**1987**	First World Cup to be held outside England (in India/ Pakistan)
Return of South Africa to cricket with an ODI in India	**1991**	
	1992	1992 World Cup: fielding restrictions, day/night matches, white balls and coloured uniforms
Saqlain Mushtaq invents the doosra	**1995**	
	1999	Duckworth-Lewis system adopted by ICC
Hansie Cronje match-fixing scandal	**2000**	
	2003	T20 cricket
ICC introduces powerplay	**2005**	
	2007	Australia complete a hat-trick as World Cup winners

2B. The CricketX Methodology

It is by logic that we prove, but by intuition that we discover. To know how to criticize is good, to know how to create is better.

~Henri Poincaré

The limited overs format makes ODI cricket outcomes noisier than those of Test cricket. To appreciate this point, one needs to look no further than the Indian Premier League (IPL)—which is even noisier—where anything can happen. There is a silver lining for ODI cricket though—since it is over in just one day, instead of five days for Test cricket, the nature of the pitch does not vary during the ODI game as much as it does in the Test game.

The problem is that there is only *one* piece of information with which to allocate credit or blame to *three* interacting factors. And that information is the team score (runs and wickets fallen) from the scorecard. Consider a hypothetical example: when New Zealand score 210 runs for 8 wickets in 50 overs against England, it is simultaneously an indication of their batting (that they scored almost 26 runs per wicket at 4.2 runs per over) and an indication of English bowling (that they gave away 26 runs for each wicket taken at 4.2 runs per over). Oh, and we shouldn't forget the effect of the pitch. So, is this score an outcome of exceptional New Zealand batting against a terrific English attack on a treacherous pitch? Or is it the result of mediocre batting strength on an easy pitch against an average pack of bowlers? The permutations are numerous.

Stated simply, the observed phenomenon of a score only tells us the interaction of three factors—i.e. batting strength, bowling strength, and pitch conditions. How do we separate the three? Let's start by discussing how the pitch matters.

Whatever model one adopts, it has to untie the following Gordian knot—my score is an outcome of my batting relative to your bowling, and your score is an outcome of your batting relative to my bowling. There are four unknowns here, and only two pieces of information to identify them—the relative performances (team scores) for each innings. To tighten this knot, the observed team scores are also affected by the pitch!

The Pitch

It is a truism that the nature of the pitch—the bounce, predictability, speed with which the ball leaves the grass or the bald turf—are indicators of whether it is easy or difficult to bat, and in a symmetric fashion, whether it is difficult or easy to bowl on. This simultaneity is also indicated by the terms that have arisen: a batting paradise is also a bowling graveyard, or a batting nightmare is a bowler's dream. It is this simultaneity that makes analysis difficult—if score is an outcome of pitch, batting and bowling, how can the impact of pitch be isolated?

We would like to compare matches unencumbered by considerations of differences in pitch. An obvious point, but one that bears emphasis, is that no single, or multiple, pitch index can capture the myriad variations that a pitch goes through during the course of a match or from match to match. But to arrive at such a precise calculation of intra-match pitch variations is not necessary. All that is needed is a method which broadly distinguishes between dead and sticky, dry and wet, paradise and nightmare.

The first and obvious method of computing a pitch index would be to group pitches by the country in which they are located. Figure 2B.1 documents the average first innings score in all complete (non-Duckworth-Lewis) matches by venue country for major cricket playing nations. Since we are looking at an average of a huge sample of matches where teams of varying batting and bowling strengths have faced each other on numerous occasions, their effects balance out and we are left with some indicator of the average pitch in that country. As expected, the easiest pitches in the world can be found in India (highest average first innings score). No wonder, therefore, that all the double centuries in ODI matches have taken place in India. On the other hand, Australian and Sri Lankan pitches are the toughest.

This method is crude but has its advantages—it is exogenous, i.e. it is not calculated from what transpires in a particular match, so it will allow for pre-match predictions. But it has its drawbacks as well—it makes the assumption that all pitches in a country are same. Clearly, that is not true.

Figure 2B.1: Venue and First Innings Scores

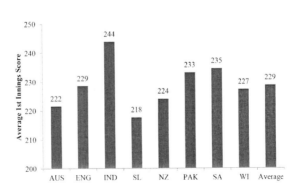

Source: CricketX database

We can refine our process by looking at the number of matches played previously on that pitch instead of a country-level grouping. Even this would not capture any abrupt changes in the pitch from its recent past, but it would be a more workable indicator. After all, perfect is the enemy of good when it comes to modelling real-world human interactions, whether it is the stock market or sports.

The Pitch Index

So now that we have decided to use previous matches held at a particular venue in order to construct our pitch index, how do we actually compute it?

For Test cricket, BTW (1987) had offered the following simple calculation of the pitch index. It was observed that the (average) total number of overs bowled in the first two innings of a Test match at Lord's was 215. By taking the Lord's pitch as our reference, the pitch index was defined as

$$\text{Test Match Pitch Index} = \frac{215}{\text{Overs bowled in the first two innings}}$$

If a pitch was easy, then more than 215 overs would be bowled in the first two innings and the index would be considerably less than one. If the pitch was difficult—all other factors (like team strengths) being equal—then considerably less than 215 overs would be bowled in the first two innings and the pitch index would be more than one. Multiplication of an individual's score by the pitch index would yield a pitch-adjusted score, the score on an average Lord's pitch.

The above definition works because it takes into account

how both the batting sides are affected—an easy pitch should make batting easier for both teams and not just one, and the first innings of the team batting second is not constrained by the number of overs or the score of the first team.

Unfortunately, such a neat definition is not possible for ODI cricket. Both teams play close to fifty overs each and the score of the second team is constrained by the target set by the team batting first. One way out is to compute the index as follows.

$$\text{ODI Match Pitch Index} = \frac{517}{\text{Test-like score for 1st inning} + \text{Test-like score for 2nd inning}}$$

For both teams we project a 'test-like score', i.e. what would have been their score had they batted for all ten wickets, and done so without any overs constraint. For example, let's assume the team batting first scored 220 for 7 in 50 overs. Now, by looking at all the ODI matches we find that the last three wickets contribute 15 per cent more runs to the existing score. So our test-like score for the first innings is 220 + 15 per cent of 220 = 253. Similarly, we compute the test-like score for the second innings. We then take the sum of these two test-like scores for each match. On average across ODI history, this sum comes out to be close to 517. We now define our pitch index relative to this global average.

The value of the ratio is the ODI match pitch index. A value of one signifies a 'neutral' or an average pitch; a value less than one, an easier pitch; a value greater than one, a difficult pitch.

How well does our pitch index capture the venue country effect? Very well indeed, as shown in Table 2B.1. India has the lowest pitch index (implying the easiest pitches) and Australia and Sri Lanka have the highest pitch index (implying difficult-to-score pitches). Additionally, one can observe the game becoming more batsmen friendly through the secular decline in the pitch index across *all* countries over time.

Table 2B.1: Pitch Index by Venue Country and Decade

Venue Country	1970s	1980s	1990s	2000s	2010s	All
AUS	1.16	1.07	1.07	0.98	0.95	1.04
ENG	1.03	0.95	0.97	0.97	0.94	0.97
IND	–	0.99	0.98	0.92	0.91	0.95
SL	–	1.17	1.01	1.06	0.96	1.04
NZ	1.10	1.09	1.06	1.01	0.94	1.03
PAK	1.20	1.05	0.98	0.91	–	0.97
SA	–	–	1.01	0.98	0.94	0.99
WI	–	1.02	0.96	1.00	1.00	0.99
Average	1.07	1.04	1.02	0.98	0.95	1.00

Source: CricketX database
Note: ODI Pitch Index = 517/(Test-like score for 1st inning + Test-like score for 2nd inning)

Time for Some Rocket Science—Kalman Filter

We have reached the first destination of our journey to 'unravel the scorecard'. The contaminating effects of the pitch have been delicately removed. What remains is to derive team strengths, batting and bowling, for each team.

For that, it is important to first recognize that team scores (after being adjusted by pitch) are a reflection of the batting strength relative to the bowling strength. The keyword here is relative. Whether it is two school teams, or two ODI teams, the ratio of their strengths determines the expected score. If the two are equal (my batting index equal to your bowling index), then the school team or an ODI team will score the same number of runs on a neutral or adjusted pitch.

How do we separate the two? It is not an easy task and we resort to some rocket science—quite literally—to accomplish this. The technique we use is a space-age technique called a Kalman filter, named after the statistician who first developed this econometric algorithm. What does a Kalman filter do? Simply put, it incorporates new information and *optimally* adjusts to it. As an oversimplified example, think of a rocket (spaceship) going to the Moon. There is an unknown 'true' path in three dimensions that the rocket should take from the Earth to the Moon. The rocket starts off in the general direction of its target. After a while, it observes that it is moving further away from the target (new observation) than towards it (prior expectation). It needs to do some course-correction by firing its engines. But how much should that boost be in x direction, how much in y direction and how much in z direction? It has to deduce the amount of correction needed in all three directions from just one piece of information— how its point-to-point distance is changing with respect to its target (Figure 2B.2). Sounds familiar? The way it resolves this seemingly intractable problem is by looking at the new series of observations jointly with the past series and then making a 'statistically' best 'triple guess', one which maximizes consistency with the old and the new data combined.

Now what if the rocket over-corrects? The same process works again—the rocket observes it has overshot and computes the required boost components again. This time an opposite boost will be delivered. This happens continuously throughout the course of the flight, thus assuring that the rocket never strays too far off from its true but unknown path.

Figure 2B.2: Working of the Kalman Filter

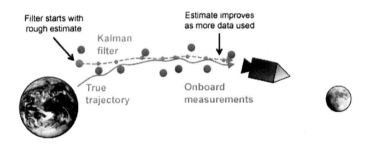

Source: http://plus.maths.org/content/understanding-unseen

Now instead of the Kalman filter honing in on the true but unknown path in three dimensions from one piece of information, think of it as honing in on the true but initially unknown bowling and batting strengths of the two teams (four dimensions) from two pieces of information. As an example, assume the two teams playing are Australia and South Africa, and they are playing on an average pitch, and there is no home team advantage (think Lord's). Assume that, to begin with, the batting and bowling strengths of the two teams are equal, at 100. As such, both South Africa and Australia should score around 230, the average first innings score on an average pitch (Figure 2B.1). An exciting match is in store. Now assume that Australia scores 50 runs below expectations, and South Africa canters to victory with five wickets to spare.

In terms of our rocket model, our course (100 for both teams) seems off the mark with regard to the new information we have. A course correction is required. Australia's batting and bowling need to be downgraded, and South Africa needs to be scaled upwards with respect to Australia (and not necessarily by the same amount). How much should this course correction be? Finding that 'optimum' amount of scaling up and down is the job of the Kalman filter. What is this optimum value? The optimum value is chosen in such a way that the updated batting, bowling and team strengths are 'statistically' most consistent with the historical outcomes plus the new observation. Therefore, each time, there will only be a small incremental correction because the updated value also needs to be consistent with the previous outcomes and not just this particular one. To bring a little bit of economics into the picture, what the Kalman filter does is a sophisticated job of modelling adaptive expectations. After this one match performance, our expectations about South Africa's batting score have gone up, and those for Australia have decreased slightly.

At any point in time, the Kalman filter gives us its best guess of the batting and bowling strengths of each team—the guess that is most consistent with all the outcomes that have been observed so far. The matches far in the past get less weight than the recently held matches—another desirable property of the model. We now have a *prior* on each team's ability to score on an average pitch. If the team scores more than this prior, then the method updates the values and predicts a slightly higher score in the next match. If the team scores less, the method downgrades the expectations for the next match. And so on.

Summarizing, the following four simple steps are involved in generating team strengths over time:

Step 1: Make the problem easier by removing the confounding effect of the pitch by constructing a pitch index. Obtain pitch-adjusted scores of each team by multiplying their scores by the computed pitch index. For example, if the score is 300, and the pitch has an index of 0.8, then the pitch adjusted score is 240.

Step 2: Before the match starts, we have a prior expectation of a team's batting strength and the opposition's bowling strength. These priors yield the expected score which can, obviously, be more than or less than the actual score.

Step 3: The difference between the expected and actual score of a team is fed into the Kalman filter, which decomposes it into the corrections required for batting and bowling strengths.

Step 4: The corrections are incorporated to get the new, updated batting and bowling strengths and we are ready with our priors for the next match.

A legitimate question can now be raised: what happens if the model foolishly upgrades a team on the basis of a fluke performance? Are all the results therefore in error?

The answer to this important question is straightforward and in two parts. First, the optimizing method prevents any large corrections. Second, even if some 'error' is made (and this will occur), in future matches the model will correct itself as the role of luck evens out. For example, suppose, due to an uncharacteristically exceptional performance, the Sri Lankan team scores 300 against Australia on a neutral pitch. Let us also assume that they were expected to score 230. The model will boost Sri Lanka's batting and downgrade Australia's bowling in such a way that the expectation from Sri Lanka in their next match against Australia will be a number greater than 230, but not all the way to 300, e.g. 242. When the next match comes along, on a normal pitch again, the Sri Lankans, unaided by luck this time, score 230—according to earlier expectations. The model will then correctly revise its estimates downwards for Sri Lanka. Fairly soon, the system will converge and the right estimate will be obtained.

> 'Data is the sword of the 21st century,
> those who wield it well, the Samurai.'
>
> ~Jonathan Rosenberg
> Senior Vice-President, Google

It's All One Big Game

There's another 'cool' innovation. Imagine India beating South Africa against expectations. The model upgrades India and downgrades South Africa by the optimum amount. Now imagine South Africa beating a strong Australia against expectations. It is obvious that at the end of the latter match

South Africa will be upgraded. Here comes the kicker—shouldn't India be upgraded too at the end of the *second* match? After all, it beat South Africa which beat a stronger Australia. It should, and it does. Again, the optimum amount of upgrade will be decided by the venerable Kalman filter. Since all estimates of team strengths are relative (hence linked), every match reveals new information about *all* teams. The impact on estimates will be the highest for the two teams that actually played the match and then slowly spread out to estimates of other teams depending on how recently they played with these two and so on, like a web, the effect dampening at every extra step.

Which leaves one final question—how does this model, start? It starts at 100 for *each* team in its first ever ODI match. And thereafter, it evolves with observed scores, and adaptive expectations. Voila! We have the answer to the seemingly intractable problem of how to observe batting and bowling strengths when both depend on each other as well as the pitch.

What Does It All Add Up To?

There is no reason why anyone should completely accept either the reasoning or the set of assumptions that have been outlined above. Some legitimate questions can be raised about any or all the assumptions. That is as it should be. But that is no reason to stop now, for as always, the proof of a method is in the results. What has been set up is a completely objective framework that leaves no room for post-fact subjective elements or expert adjustments. *Untouched by human hands* would be an apt description. This may seem cold and/or unrealistic and/or naive. Perhaps it is, but if the model and/or its assumptions are wrong or more correctly not useful (as all assumptions by definition are wrong—otherwise they would be called facts), then the error will show up in the results. So, with the help of rocket science, how much of ODI cricket has our CricketX model been able to predict?

2C. How Good Is the CricketX Model?

Essentially, all models are wrong. Some are useful.

~George E.P. Box

So far, we have outlined a statistical model that measures batting and bowling (and team) strengths from the match scorecard and predicts ODI outcomes. The act of prediction is important and not just for entertainment, because it gives us a way to evaluate the evaluators—be it a statistical model or a human expert. A model or an expert that is correct 60 per cent of the time is using information in a more meaningful way than one that is correct only 55 per cent of the time and hence, the results from the former are more authentic than the results from the latter.

So how accurate are CricketX's predictions? Across all ODI matches played between the top ten cricket teams (the eight Test playing nations—Australia, England, India, Sri Lanka, New Zealand, Pakistan, South Africa, West Indies—and two others—Zimbabwe and Bangladesh), CricketX has picked the winner correctly 65 per cent of the time. In World Cup matches, the accuracy has been higher at 72 per cent, but that's a discussion for another chapter. For now, let us examine this seemingly pedestrian 65 per cent accuracy rate (Figure 2C.1, Figure 2C.2).

Figure 2C.1: CricketX Forecast Accuracy by Decade

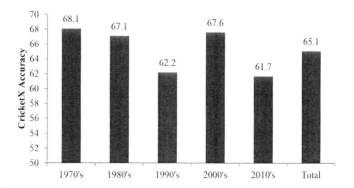

Source: CricketX database

Figure 2C.2: CricketX Forecast Accuracy by Team

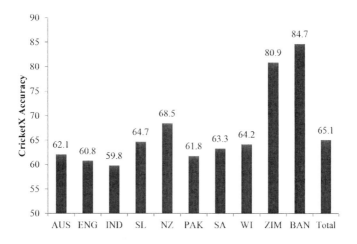

Source: CricketX database

A 65 per cent accuracy rate seems to be better than what one can achieve in the stock markets, but worse than what is possible in chess. And that is how it should be. Predicting the behaviour of two people (chess) should be easier than predicting that of 22 (cricket), which in turn should be easier than predicting the behaviour of millions (stock markets). Also, remember that the model is not allowed to pick its spots—it is judged across all matches.

Maybe you are still unimpressed. After all, you have religiously followed the sport over the past decade, and given that every year close to 1,500 hours of international cricket are played, you are well over Canadian journalist and author Malcolm Gladwell's prescriptive 10,000 hours of practice needed to be an expert. You think you (or that cricket-junkie friend of yours) can easily beat that paltry 65 per cent accuracy.

Consider this—Bangladesh has won about 23 per cent of its matches. Now, in how many of those would you have put your money on Bangladesh before the match started? *Close to none.* If an inexperienced team like Bangladesh can forge setbacks so 'often', what about the stronger teams?

We looked at outcomes of all head-to-head series of three or more matches across the history of ODI cricket. The winner (the team that won more matches in the series) won 77 per cent of its games, i.e. the result of a five-match series is more 4-1 than 5-0. (Interestingly, this too gives us the same fraction of upsets as provided by the Bangladesh example—23 per cent.) Therefore, even if you had a crystal ball that could predict the winner of each series with 100 per cent accuracy, your overall hit rate of each match would be only 77 per cent.

Letter written by a young 'cricket-fanatic' to Surjit Bhalla after the release of his book *Between the Wickets: The Who and Why of the Best in Cricket*. As it turns out, the young Benedict is today a senior cricket statistician at Sky Sports.

Dear Dr. Bhalla,

I am fourteen years old and I am a cricket fanatic, and I enjoy playing imaginary games of cricket with dice, cards, and a whole host of other methods.

A few months ago, there was an article in our newspaper, The Daily Telegraph, about your talk at the London School of Economics on 'A case study of Test Cricket', in which you explained your computer-aided comparison of all Test players and teams since the advent of Test cricket in 1877.

I enjoy producing my own ratings, but I only have the players' averages to go by. You, similarly, have a great advantage with the use of computers.

I recently discovered that you had written a book on your findings, and I would greatly appreciate it if you could let me know where I would obtain it from in England, if anywhere, and if you would send me some of matches in your ratings.

Yours sincerely,
Benedict Bermange.

But surely, there are some upsets at the series level too. Obvious recent examples include Bangladesh beating New Zealand 3-0 in November 2013; around the same time South Africa beat Pakistan 4-1 in the United Arab Emirates and then immediately lost 2-1 at home—one of these two South Africa–Pakistan series has to be counted as an upset. More such examples can be found. Simple arithmetic shows that you need to be wrong in only one out of six series for your overall accuracy to drop to 65 per cent! Not so unimpressive now, is it? Keep in mind that you have to pick winners for all the series and not just those that you feel most confident about—which means picking a side even when you feel the situation is too close to call.

The fact that even simple statistical models outperform human experts is well documented. Philip Tetlock's *Expert Political Judgment: How Good Is it? How Can We Know?* (2005) describes a twenty-year study in which 284 experts in many fields, including government officials, professors, journalists, and others, with divergent views, were asked to make 28,000 predictions about the future. It was found that the experts were only slightly more accurate than chance, and worse than basic computer algorithms (Wikipedia). Grove et al. (2000) conducted a meta-analysis—a fancy word for a study of studies—on 136 published studies that analysed the accuracy of computers/models v the judgement of human experts. These studies spanned a wide range of fields from predicting academic performance to criminal behaviour to medical diagnosis. Their result: models beat or equal experts in 94 per cent of the studies.

How is this possible? It is because humans suffer from a number of cognitive biases. Daniel Kahneman, a psychologist who won the Nobel prize for Economics in 2002 for his extensive work on the psychology of judgement and decision-making, has documented a number of such biases in his excellent book *Thinking, Fast and Slow*.

> *The only relevant test of the validity of a hypothesis is comparison of prediction with experience.*
>
> ~Milton Friedman

It turns out that we tend to apply our knowledge *inconsistently*, coming to a different conclusion with the same facts on a different occasion. We also tend to believe in stories without bothering to examine empirical evidence in support of them. To top it all, we are generally overconfident about our abilities, even after being wrong. Indeed, while retrospecting, we tend to count our 'near misses' as 'hits' and do so with impunity, without even being aware that we are doing so. Models, on the other hand, contain the knowledge of experts who built them and are free from such biases, in application of that knowledge.

The humble 65 per cent looks respectable now, and indeed it is. It also bears testimony to the dynamism and uncertainty inherent in the game itself. The unpredictability is good for it keeps the sport exciting. If ODI matches were highly predictable, there would be no point in playing them. The major ODI teams are rarely more than 20 per cent apart in overall strength. Hence it should come as no surprise that most of the contests have odds in the 60–40 range. Note that a 60 per cent chance of winning for the stronger team implies that it is likely to lose four out of ten times. The possibility of the underdog winning is always real and the audience always has a chance to be thrilled and inspired.

So, in terms of accuracy, our statistical model is definitely a consistent, unbiased and untiring stand-in for a very astute human expert with a proven track record, if not better (the odds are that it is much better). Now that we have established this 'fact', we are in a position to tackle the most interesting and vexing questions of ODI cricket with a great deal of confidence: Which have been the greatest and worst teams in cricket history? Who are ODI's best and greatest batsmen, bowlers and all-rounders? What counts for more in a batsman—strike rate or batting average? And by how much? What about the relative importance of economy for the bowler? How does one isolate the contribution of captains from the strength of the teams they lead?

These and additional questions are addressed (no fence-sitting) in the remainder of the book. In essence, the system has given itself a long enough rope. The reader can now object to the *reality* of the results, as opposed to debating its theory. The challenge is there for both CricketX and the reader—the former to make itself acceptable and respectable, and the latter to have an open mind towards being convinced. Let reality win.

3

TEAMS—*WHOLE* > Σ *PARTS*

One equal temper of heroic hearts,
Made weak by time and fate, but strong in will,
To strive, to seek, to find, and not to yield.

~Alfred Tennyson, *Ulysses*

Numerous authoritative commentators have spilled ink over comparisons between players and teams, so we are in good company—of people who do care. Sobers, in his autobiography *Twenty Years at the Top*, goes through a detailed comparison between the West Indies teams of 1963 and 1986 and concludes that the 1963 team was better. Just to jog your memory, the 1963 West Indies team had the likes of Frank Worrell, Garfield Sobers, Conrad Hunte, Rohan Kanhai, Wes Hall, Charlie Griffith and Lance Gibbs. The 1983 team, not to be outdone so easily (but outdone!), had Clive Lloyd, Gordon Greenidge, Viv Richards, Malcolm Marshall, Andy Roberts and Michael Holding. Tom Graveney (along with Norman Giller) in *The Ten Greatest Test Teams* unabashedly sets about the task of comparing the greatest Test teams in the post-World War II era. Kenneth Gregory in his anthology *The Celebration of*

Cricket compares the players from the 1970s to the Golden Age of cricket (1890–1914), and finds contemporary players (and teams) wanting in many respects. Add to these books the fact that every writer on cricket (including the dean, John Arlott) passes comparative judgements on players and teams, and passes them frequently, and one is led to the inescapable conclusion: *compare or be irrelevant*.

We all compare. In fact, isn't all of sport just that—an elaborate attempt to compare an individual or a group against another. Comparisons made by observers of the game are not just about indulging some innate human need for speculation; they are mandatory. Mandatory because comparisons help, and improve understanding.

But on what basis do we compare the teams and players? We should only compare them based on what they strive to achieve during the course of a game—victory. An American football coach, George Allen, said that with each loss he died a little. Appropriately, the French say that with each broken love affair, they die a little. Actually, the two claimants are not that far apart—only the objects of their affection are different.

Winning is terribly important, though it is alleged that in cricket, it is only a recent obsession. However, the allegation does not have enough support, for the assumption that the gentleman's sport is played for fun and a few marbles is a relic for the historians. English captain Douglas Jardine did not indulge in 'Bodyline' to test the market for a new brassiere; and Clive Lloyd did not harness the 'Four Horsemen of the Apocalypse' (Garner, Holding, Marshall, Roberts) to test the ability of batsmen to breakdance on a cricket pitch.

A central theme, then, pertaining to any analysis of cricket, is that it revolves around victory. A team adjudged to be better than another should have a higher chance of beating it than being beaten by it. Similarly, a player adjudged better than another should increase the chances of his team winning, all else being equal.

Now, winning may be the goal and perhaps even the raison d'être, of modern-day cricket, but win/loss records cannot be used, by themselves, to measure team strengths accurately. Why? There are several confounding factors. Not all wins are created equal. A win against a strong team should count for more than a win against a weak team. A win at home should count for less than a win abroad, because common sense says, and the data confirms, that a considerable home team advantage exists. Similarly, successfully chasing a large total with eight wickets to spare is indicative of greater talent than scampering to make it to an average target.

We need to construct an indicator of team talent, or strength, which accounts for all these factors. And we will, but for now let us start by examining the 'raw' or unadjusted data—data which have not been processed by our model—to get the big picture.

Table 3.1 documents the winning record for each country and the overall record clearly suggests that Australia and South Africa have been the most successful nations in ODI cricket. We now make an important distinction between a country and a team, relevant mostly to this chapter (in the subsequent chapters, the terms are used interchangeably and their meaning is clear from the context). A team belongs to a country and to an era; for example, the Indian team today is different from the Indian team ten years ago which in turn is very different from the one that won the World Cup in 1983. Therefore, we need to break down the win record of the countries into several periods in order to zero in on the best team in cricketing history. Hence, Table 3.1 also presents decade-wise win records of all countries.

Table 3.1: Team Summary and Win Percentage by Decade

	AUS	ENG	IND	SL	NZ	PAK	SA	WI	ZIM	BAN
Mat	813	605	830	700	623	806	508	695	425	287
Wins	518	303	437	345	282	438	322	369	113	82
Losses	295	302	393	355	341	368	186	326	312	205
Tied	9	7	7	4	6	8	6	8	5	0
Win %	64	50	53	49	45	54	63	53	27	29
Win % by Decade										
1970s	50	64	15	20	47	40.0	–	74	–	–
1980s	51	53	46	21	46	49	–	72	8	0
1990s	66	46	50	48	40	57	64	51	29	9
2000s	75	47	55	58	50	58	64	43	26	30
2010s	64	53	63	55	42	51	62	41	29	35

Source: CricketX database, as of 23 November 2014
Note: Number of matches and win percentage exclude no-result matches, and ties are counted as half a win.

Now, things get more interesting and two strong contenders emerge—the West Indies team of the 1970s and 1980s and the Australia team of the 2000s. Both teams won more than 70 per cent of their matches and the record of Australia in 2000s at 75 per cent is a tad better than that of West Indies in the 1970s and 1980s. Is that enough for us to pronounce Australia the greatest team? No. First, the difference is small and could just be an artefact of the way we have sliced up the 45 years of history. Second, we need to make a correction for the confounding factors discussed earlier. What if West Indies were battling stronger opponents more often and winning more emphatically than Australia was?

It is time to enlist the services of our CricketX model, outlined in Chapter 2. For every match, CricketX adjusts for pitch differences using a pre-computed pitch index and then looks at the margin of victory after adjusting it for the strength of the opposition. Prior team strengths and the observed margin of victory are then fed into the Kalman filter, which yields the updated team strengths after making optimal adjustments to reflect the new information. These team indices at any point in time then reflect the statistically best estimate of the teams' underlying true strength after having been corrected for the confounding factors noted earlier (including home team advantage). How do we know that CricketX has done a good job and these team indices are indeed what they claim to be? By its ability to predict. As shown in Chapter 2C, these CricketX team indices correctly forecast a very admirable 65 per cent of the ODI outcomes. We can now wield the indices with a significant degree of confidence.

> *'The way a team plays as a whole determines its success. You may have the greatest bunch of individual stars in the world, but if they don't play together, the club won't be worth a dime.'*
>
> ~Babe Ruth

What do these mystical CricketX indices look like? The batting (CxBat), bowling (CxBowl) and team indices (CxTeam) are all indexed to 100, which simply means that a value of 100 for the index represents an average through the history of ODI cricket. A team with a CxBat of 100 has an average batting strength, and a team with a CxBowl of 100 has an average bowling line-up. It is quite possible, and is indeed frequent, for a team to be average in one department and above (or below) average in the other. Even an average team (CxTeam of 100) can have batting and bowling strengths that are different than 100.

The CricketX model endows these indices with several interesting statistical properties. A team with a CxTeam of 110 is 10 per cent better than the average ODI team. Better in a very real tangible sense. The indices have been constructed in such a way that their values reflect the productivity of the team in scoring or saving runs—the final arbiter and the ultimate goal of every act undertaken in ODI cricket. So, a team with a CxTeam of 110 is expected to score about 10 per cent more runs than the average ODI team. When a team with a CxBat of 100 plays against a team with a CxBowl of 100, one can expect an average first innings ODI score of 230. When a team with a CxBat of 110 plays a team with CxBowl of 100, it can be expected to score 10 per cent more runs than the average ODI first innings score, or 230 + 23 = 253. In this way, the indices at any point in time give us a ranking, and also tell us how good or bad each team is in very concrete terms.

Table 3.2 and Figure 3.1 provide an overview of the three CricketX indices for different terms for two periods, 1990-2009 and since 2010. For the recent period, note how effectively the indices bring out the batting-dependence of India, the bowling tilt of Pakistan and the balance in teams of Australia and South Africa.

Table 3.2: Average Batting (CxBat), Bowling (CxBowl) and Team (CxTeam) Indices for Teams since 1990

Team	1990-2009			2010-Present		
	CxTeam	CxBat	CxBowl	CxTeam	CxBat	CxBowl
AUS	114	110	102	108	105	104
ENG	104	99	105	102	102	95
IND	103	101	98	105	105	97
SL	105	99	105	106	101	104
NZ	102	96	105	99	95	104
PAK	104	103	100	103	100	105
SA	107	99	107	108	105	104
WI	101	97	104	94	95	95
ZIM	83	89	93	77	82	88
BAN	73	76	90	85	91	91

Source: CricketX database

Figure 3.1: Average Batting (CxBat), Bowling (CxBowl) and Team (CxTeam) Indices for Top 8 Teams since 2010

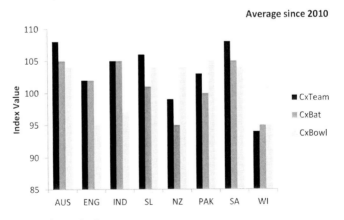

Source: CricketX database

Back to the business of finding the best team. Armed with such indices, it is tempting to simply look at which team achieved the highest value of CxTeam in ODI history and pronounce it the winner. This would indeed represent the highest peak achieved in ODI cricket, and in a sense, that team can be called the best team. It would have been on a massive domination streak, not possible by luck alone. If you were asked to pick any team from any point in history to represent you in a crucial match, that team should be your unambiguous choice.

So are we done? Not yet. For there is the best and then, there are the greatest. There is a distinction between the two that we understand implicitly. 'Greatest' has a ring of longevity to it, an extended period of dominance. The best need to conquer time before they become the greatest. This applies to teams as well as their players—when we compare batsmen and bowlers in the subsequent chapters, we will place this additional hurdle of conquering time before anointing them the greatest. How do we then quantify greatness in cricket?

Here is our stab at it. At the very least, we need to know who was number one and for how long. For this, we go back in history and rank all the teams every year by their average team index—CxTeam—for that year. Table 3.3 presents these rankings along with the total number of ODI matches played in that year.

This 'map' tells the story of ODI cricket since its inception. It shows the leading teams in ODI history and how the baton has been passing from one to the other. The West Indies had the best team from inception (circa 1975, by which time every major team had played at least one ODI match) till 1989;

in 1990 the West Indies' dominance ended and a period of upheaval ensued. Several teams ascended to the number one spot, only to be dethroned the following year. There was Pakistan in 1990; England flashed to number one in 1992 and were the favoured team to win the World Cup that year—however, they lost the final to Pakistan who were ranked number five. The West Indies made a brief comeback but it did not last long. South Africa and Sri Lanka also made transient appearances—a veritable Game of Thrones. It all ended with the rise of the Australians, the Wizards of Oz. Their dominance was almost absolute for a decade, like the West Indies, but now they might be waning. A new superpower in the form of South Africa is in ascendance—will they claim this decade? Only time will tell.

The evolution of the ranks in the table confirms most experts' rankings of the teams and tallies with our earlier observation of the raw data—a rather robust confirmation of our model. At such a macro level of analysis, the CricketX model should not be at loggerheads with the general assessment.

Table 3.3: Game of Thrones—Team Rankings by Year

Year	AUS	ENG	IND	SL	NZ	PAK	SA	WI	ZIM	BAN	Total Matches
1971	1	2									1
1972	1	2									3
1973	2	3			4	5		1			4
1974	2	3	4		5	6		1			6
1975	2	3	5	6	7	4		1			14
1976	2	4	7	6	5	3		1			6
1977	2	4	7	6	5	3		1			6
1978	2	3	7	6	5	4		1			8
1979	3	2	6	7	4	5		1			21
1980	5	2	6	7	3	4		1			21
1981	4	3	6	7	2	5		1			27
1982	3	4	6	7	2	5		1			28
1983	6	3	4	8	2	5		1	7		62
1984	2	4	3	8	5	6		1	7		46
1985	3	4	2	8	6	5		1	7		62
1986	4	6	3	8	5	2		1	7	9	56
1987	4	2	5	7	6	3		1	8	9	73
1988	3	1	4	7	6	5		2	8	9	61
1989	5	2	6	7	4	3		1	8	9	52
1990	2	5	6	7	4	1		3	8	9	57
1991	1	5	6	8	3	2	7	4	9	10	38
1992	3	1	4	8	6	5	7	2	9	10	77
1993	2	4	6	8	7	3	5	1	9	10	75
1994	2	5	6	7	8	3	4	1	9	10	84
1995	1	4	5	6	8	7	3	2	9	10	57
1996	3	8	5	2	7	6	1	4	9	10	104

Year	AUS	ENG	IND	SL	NZ	PAK	SA	WI	ZIM	BAN	Total Matches
1997	7	8	3	1	6	2	5	4	9	10	97
1998	4	3	5	7	9	6	1	2	8	10	99
1999	2	8	3	7	5	4	1	6	9	10	123
2000	1	6	7	4	5	2	3	8	9	10	122
2001	1	7	6	4	5	3	2	8	9	10	103
2002	1	5	7	3	6	4	2	8	9	10	120
2003	1	2	6	4	8	7	3	5	9	10	105
2004	1	3	4	2	5	7	6	8	9	10	109
2005	1	3	7	6	4	2	5	8	10	9	91
2006	1	6	3	2	4	7	5	8	10	9	112
2007	1	5	6	3	2	8	4	7	10	9	112
2008	1	6	3	4	2	8	5	7	9	10	75
2009	2	6	1	4	3	5	7	8	10	9	103
2010	1	6	7	4	3	2	5	8	10	9	93
2011	1	6	4	3	7	5	2	8	10	9	95
2012	4	7	2	3	8	5	1	6	10	9	66
2013	5	3	1	4	6	7	2	8	10	9	96
2014	4	5	3	2	7	6	1	8	10	9	67

Source: CricketX database

West Indies 1975–1989 or Australia 1999–2011—Head to Head

The search for the greatest ODI team ends with one of these two—the Lloyd–Richards West Indies team of the 1970s and 1980s or the Waugh–Ponting Australia team of 1999–2011. To be sure, there were very few matches played in the earlier years of ODI cricket, but the longer sway of the West Indies made up for that. In fact, this is the reason why even though West Indies dominated for a longer period, we cannot decide in their favour. Let us see if CricketX can help decide.

Table 3.4 presents several head-to-head comparisons of the two teams for their respective eras of dominance. The win percentage as observed earlier is very close—72.6 per cent for West Indies v 73.6 per cent for Australia. The average CxTeam index for the West Indies is 114.3, lower than Australia's 117.9. CricketX rightly points out the reason for the West Indies dominance—its lethal bowling attack with a CxBowl of 115. In contrast, Australia is more batting-heavy, reflecting the trend of modern ODI cricket. What about peak performance? This squarely belongs to the Australians. They made a massive peak of 144 CxTeam points in 2003 at the back of a mind-boggling record streak of 21 consecutive wins (January to March 2003: six wins before the World Cup, eleven in the World Cup and four after it). They won most, if not all, of their matches emphatically. West Indies also had their streak but only half as long—eleven ODIs from June 1984 to February 1985. Interestingly, the West Indian juggernaut was stopped by Australia and the Australian streak ended because of the West Indies.

So far, except for peak performances, the differences are small but in favour of Australia. One final important detail remains. In such cross-era comparisons, it is imperative to think about the advances in technology, equipment and fitness levels that benefit the modern players. While it is impossible to accurately compensate for advances in technology, one can use some useful proxies—usually something that reflects the level of other good teams and players of that era. In our case, we can look at how far ahead these two teams were from the second best teams of their era. Here again, the two are close—West Indies was on average 7.4 per cent better than the teams ranked second during 1975–89 and Australia was 8.1 per cent better than the second-in-command during 1999–2011.

Table 3.4: Who Is the Greatest? West Indies v Australia

		West Indies 1975–89	Australia 1999–2011
Matches		191	370
Win %		72.6	73.6
Average			
	CxTeam	114.3	117.9
	CxBat	102.8	112.8
	CxBowl	115.1	105.6
Peak			
	CxTeam	125.4	144.0
Distance			
From Rank 2		7.4	8.1

Source: CricketX database

So who is the greatest? While both these great teams are very close on most parameters, Australia does hold a faint edge over West Indies. We asked CricketX what would be the outcome of a hypothetical match between these two sultans of ODI cricket. It grimaced but obliged—53-47 in favour of Australia. Oh, what a match that would be!

4

BATSMEN—THE FAVOURED

Greatness is beauty with a difference—it is not only in the eyes of the beholder.

~Surjit

Everybody has a favourite batsman, after Don Bradman, of course. South Africa produced some stars before 1970—Barry Richards will go down in history as the greatest post-War Test batsman the world never knew, and Graeme Pollock earned the right to compete for the title of the best after Bradman. For ODI cricket, the names that immediately come to mind are Vivian Richards, Sachin Tendulkar and Sanath Jayasuriya. A verification of any ranking is that these three be among the prime contenders. We shall soon see whether CricketX passes this smell test. If it fails, we will be asked by you, the reader, to go back to the drawing board.

Even though we have our priors, we are here to choose the best batsmen on an objective statistical basis. But isn't every statistical truth also a manipulation? Perhaps. But as long as, and to the extent 'manipulation' can be used to predict the real world and its record verified, it should be accepted, nay celebrated. And if you thought that it is only useful for socially 'unproductive' activities like betting, know that it is the rigorous application of statistics that enables you to secure the future of your loved ones through insurance.

Coming back to cricket, we have all been brought up on a steady diet of averages being the be-all and end-all of evaluation. BTW, published as far back as 1987, contained an alternate metric (perhaps the first such), which held a few surprises. Of course, Bradman stayed number one, but the second greatest batsman, Jack Hobbs, with an average of 56.9, was ranked well ahead of his opening partner, Herb Sutcliffe (average 60.7, rank 6). This is what one of the best cricket commentators, John Arlott, had to say about Jack Hobbs: 'Others scored faster; hit the ball harder; more obviously murdered bowling. No one else, though, ever batted with more consummate skill.' There were other divergences with the traditional data and averages. Peter May, with an average of 46.8, would have ended with a rank below thirty with conventional averages; the adjusted BTW average (adjusted for pitch, opposition faced, etc.) ranked him fifteen.

Also in the 1980s, in baseball, Test cricket's second cousin and ODI cricket's first, a statistician named Billy James was writing about how conventional statistics and subjective expert judgements of a player are often in error while proposing new and better statistically rigorous measures to analyse a player's value. Some twenty years after BTW, Michael Lewis's *Moneyball* exploded on the baseball, and world stage, with the story of a Billy Beane. Beane, the general manager of the financially constrained Oakland Athletics team, inspired by James's work and mentored by his predecessor, applied sabermetrics

John Arlott's review of *Between the Wickets: The Who and Why of the Best in Cricket*

Arlott one.

Beyond the Wickets is as intriguing a cricket book as has come anyone's way, at any time. Four impressions are instantly sharp. The first, that, if ever a game seemed most certainly not to be susceptible to the judgement of the computer, it ~~must be~~ *was* cricket. Second that, if virtually everything in the world is now computerized, why should cricket not be susceptible?Thirdly, there is barely a point of relative merit between cricketers on which the closest followers of the game can agree. Fourthly, Mr. Bhalla's method is at least completely free from the normal cricket critic's besetting fault of loyalty to one particular player, club or country.

Therefore, he does all those who think and argue about cricket, a service. Let us check our prejudices by these computerized judgements. This writer thinks Sir Jack Hobbs was a greater batsman than Sir Donald Bradman because he was so much more consistently effective on difficult batting wickets. Perhaps the computer machine will try to appreciate that fact: but, alas it will not say so.

This is *nevertheless,* a salutary and illuminating book, on which Mr. Bhalla is to be congratulated: and which will humble all of us who love and dispute about the game we never thought could be mechanically assessed.

(the statistical study of baseball) to turn Oakland Athletics into the most cost-effective team in baseball. In 2002, Athletics became the first team in the 100-plus years of American League baseball to win twenty consecutive games. In the 2006 season, Athletics ranked 24 out of 30 major league teams in player salaries but had the fifth best regular-season record. In the same year, *Time* magazine named James in the Time 100 Most Influential People list. Where is cricket's Billy Beane?

Valuing a Batsman: The Bottom-up Way

In Chapter 2, we discussed how any observed batting outcome is a function of batting skill, bowling faced and pitch conditions. By using a pitch index, we converted actual scores to pitch-adjusted scores and then enlisted the Kalman filter to disentangle the result into batting and bowling components. This was done at a team level, and we obtained the batting (CxBat), bowling (CxBowl) and team (CxTeam) indices for each team for all matches. We now want to use these team-level indices and individual batting statistics to rank batsmen.

Which batting statistics (batting average? number of boundaries?) should be used and how should they be combined? Whichever indicators we choose to use and however we combine them, the result should be able to explain and predict future outcomes with a reasonable degree of accuracy—the higher the better. This prevents arbitrary choices of indicators and weights. We can only keep what helps to predict. If it does not, irrespective of how important we think it is, it must be discarded.

Now we know that the team indices do predict outcomes

reasonably well and the batting index (CxBat) is a good reflection of a team's batting strength. But a team is a collection of players and its batting strength is a reflection of its batsmen. So one should be able to aggregate individual statistics (adjusted for pitch and opposition) of a team's batsmen and arrive at some form of batting strength for the team. Let us call the batting strength derived this way a micro or 'bottom-up' batting strength. An example of this would be to look at all the players in a team and add up their career total of runs scored.

How do we know this is a meaningful number? We test it against something we already know is meaningful—CxBat. If our bottom-up aggregate can explain CxBat, i.e. higher values of the 'bottom-up' aggregate are associated with higher values of CxBat and lower values of the 'bottom-up' aggregate are associated with lower values of CxBat, then it is time to say 'Eureka!' We can then add 'total runs scored in career' in our toolkit as a useful metric in ranking players. We can now select players with higher total runs scored to play for our team. Doing so will increase our team's CxBat which in turn will increase our probability of winning. What if our bottom-up aggregate does not explain CxBat? Then we need to dump it, and not factor 'total runs scored in career' in our ranking process and ask for proof from those who do.

Greg Thomas was bowling to Viv Richards in a county game. Viv missed a superb outswinger, and Thomas said, *'It's red, round and weighs about 5 ounces.'*

Next ball, Viv hit Greg Thomas out of the ground and replied, *'Greg, you know what it looks like. Go ahead and find it!'*

This answers our question of which individual batting statistics to choose—we choose those that upon aggregation correlate with CxBat—the stronger the correlation, the better the worth of that indicator. Now how do we decide how much weight to give to each indicator? We give them the same weight that their aggregates get in explaining CxBat. By using *regression,* a common statistical technique to quantify dependence of one variable on another, we obtain the optimal weights for each of the indicators that we have chosen. (Incidentally, the same regression also tells us if what we have chosen is statistically significant in explaining CxBat or not.) We now use these weights to combine the individual statistics of batsmen, and there we have it—our batting strength index for batsmen. For convenience, we will refer to this too as CxBat, and it will be clear from the context whether we mean CxBat for a team or an individual.

The same ideas and methodology will be used in the next chapter to rank bowlers as well, but with CxBowl as the object of our attention.

The Importance of Ranking

Why are we doing all this? And that too with so much rigour? Is it just to find who is the best in the history of ODI cricket? Not really. We are doing this to answer a very real, daunting and frequently occurring question and one that needs to be answered well—how to compare players in real time and how to select a team. Once we have identified our indicators, we can use them to compare batsmen for their batting strength at any point in time, including today, and select the best from those available to represent our country or our club. The batsman who ranks higher will add greater value to the batting strength of a team than one who ranks lower, on average of course.

The Indicators

After putting several measures of individual batting performance through the hoops described above, we finally came up with three that are the most significant (but not equally so): batting average for the last thirty innings, strike rate for the last thirty innings and something called MES that we invented (more on this in a bit).

Why the last thirty innings and not twenty or forty, or even the entire career? Because aggregating the statistics over thirty innings gives us the best 'explanatory power', or 'fit' with respect to CxBat. Using the last twenty or forty innings also works well and gives about the same results, but with a slightly lower explanatory power. In a sense, this also answers the question of how far back you should look to compute a player's form while deciding to keep or drop him. Seems like all the hard work we did is now paying off.

A quick note on the adjustments that we make to individual batting statistics before using them to compute the batsman's CxBat. There are two adjustments to be made—for pitch and quality of bowling faced. This is straightforward as we already have the pitch index and the opposition's CxBowl for each match in which the batsman played. For each batsman's inning, we take his raw score and multiply it by the pitch index, which adjusts it upwards if the pitch was difficult, or downwards if the pitch was easy. We then take the pitch-adjusted score and multiply it by (CxBowl/100) of the bowling team, which adjusts it upwards if it was a better-than-average bowling attack (CxBowl>100), or downwards if it was a poor one (CxBowl<100). These adjustments convert the conventional, or raw or unadjusted, batting average and strike rate to an adjusted batting average and strike rate respectively.

With all this background, now we are ready to look at our third indicator, the MES.

What Is Your MES?

The MES or the *Match Equivalent Score* of a batsman is an interesting statistic. It is the minimum of two hypothetical 'scores'.

Think that only one batsman bats through the entire innings. An ODI innings typically ends before all ten wickets have fallen, the average is eight. Hence, the one-batsman innings ends when either he loses his wicket eight times—or when he has played 50 overs or 300 balls—whichever happens first. This is, in essence, the ODI format. The score at the end of this hypothetical innings is that batsman's MES.

How can we compute it? If he gets out eight times, his expected score will be his batting average multiplied by eight. If he bats for all fifty overs, his expected score will be his strike rate multiplied by three (since strike rate is expressed as runs per 100 balls). The smaller of the two scores will be reached first since our one-batsman innings would have ended then.

*MES = Minimum (Strike Rate * 3, Batting Average * 8)*

Match Equivalent Score (MES): Combining the Strike Rate with Batting Average for Batsmen in ODIs

$$\text{MES} = \text{Minimum of} \begin{cases} \text{Strike Rate} * 3 \\ \text{Batting Average} * 8 \end{cases}$$

How to quickly evaluate a batsman's ability? Calculate the MES and you have a measure which closely mirrors all the complicated math of CricketX.

Let us take the example of two distinguished batsmen, Virender Sehwag of India and Kevin Pietersen of England. Both unadjusted and adjusted data are presented. In terms of unadjusted data, Sehwag has a much better strike rate (104.3 v 86.6) but a much lower average (35.1 v 40.7). Now let us look at their MES as well. Sehwag's strike rate of 104.3 allows him to score 104.3 * 3 = 313 runs if he plays all fifty overs, but because of his batting average he would have lost eight wickets before that, by the time he scores 35.1 * 8 = 281 runs to be exact. So Sehwag's MES is 281.

Batsman	SR	Avg	SR*3	Avg*8	MES
Unadjusted					
Virender Sehwag	104.3	35.1	313	281	281
Kevin Pietersen	86.6	40.7	260	326	260
Adjusted					
Virender Sehwag	89.9	30.1	270	241	241
Kevin Pietersen	75.7	38.7	227	310	227

MES = Minimum (SR * 3, Avg * 8)

Doing the same computation for Pietersen gives his MES as 260, 21 runs less than Sehwag. In other words, if all the batsmen were Sehwag in the team, the team would score 281 runs, while an all-Pietersen team would score 21 runs less. Adjusting the data for quality of opposition and pitch, Sehwag's average falls to 30.1, somewhat greater than Pietersen's decline to 38.7. The gap between their MES declines from 21 runs to 14 runs, but the all-Sehwag team still scores more runs, thus he is a more valuable batsman by looking at MES alone.

It is interesting to reflect on what MES does. It takes a

batsman's strike rate and average and combines them, according to the ODI format, where an innings is over either when you lose all your wickets or bat all fifty overs, whichever happens first.

It is important to reiterate here that MES is not included in our indicators because its construction makes sense. It is included because it works, i.e. it improves explanatory power over and above just the strike rate and batting average. Future indicators (yes, we hope to find more) will now have to improve explanatory power over all three to get included as a factor in valuing a batsman.

The Batting Index (CxBat) for Batsmen

The three indicators, strike rate, batting average and MES, after adjustments for pitch and quality of bowling faced, are fed into a regression framework to yield one composite index of batting—the CxBat for batsmen. The regression framework also works out what combination of them works the best and the relative importance of each.

Which Is More Important—Strike Rate or Batting Average?

This question lies at the heart of several conventional rankings. Every such ranking makes an *assumption* about the relative importance of the two. Some analysts give them equal weight and add them up while coming up with a combined rank; some have even multiplied them together, all of them calling upon 'common sense' to vouch for them. We now have a definitive answer to this, and with a model to testify for it.

It turns out that while they are both important, neither is as important as a batsman's MES!

We can make sense of it this way: for a batsman having a high strike rate of 100 but very low batting average of 20, what will make him more valuable? A higher strike rate or a higher average? Obviously, a higher average. Now think of the flip case. So, the relative importance of the two to some extent depends on what a batsman's values of strike rate and batting average are. This happens because of the limited overs format of the game, which is what MES captures.

To be sure, both batting average and strike rate add value *beyond* MES. However, their effect is lessened once MES is taken into account because MES is already doing a good job of combining them. Usually, but not always, a higher CxBat is associated with a higher MES.

MES can be readily computed by just looking at the batting average and strike rate. MES is the quick and dirty answer to the question of how to combine strike rate and batting average, the long and clean one being CxBat itself. For those of you who still want a ratio for the two, we can find one by looking at how MES changes with change in either batting average or strike rate, on average. And that ratio is close to 2:1, i.e. a 10 per cent increase in strike rate is *twice* as valuable as a 10 per cent increase in batting average

The Rankings

The three representations of a batsman's value—strike rate, average and MES—while related to each other reflect separate aspects of batsmanship; and we have developed a rigorous

What is More Important—
Strike Rate or Batting Average?

*The (percentage) differences in Strike Rates are about **twice** as important as the (percentage) differences in Batting Averages.*

The same holds true for Economy v Bowling Average for bowlers—batting-bowling equivalence.

system to rank the batsmen at any point in time. We can now identify who are the best batsmen today (and such a list is presented at the end of the chapter), or who were the best a year ago or five years ago. As such, we have solved the daunting task of how to rank players in real time, which can help in team selections.

However, this is not the same as solving our original puzzle—who is the all-time best? When one has to rank players at any point in time, the objective is precise—who are the players that one can select *today* to maximize one's team's batting strength. But when one has to compare a player's entire career with that of another's, what does that mean? We surely don't mean which of the two was a better player at the end of his career. We wish to somehow compare them throughout their respective careers. One method could be to feed their career averages (strike rate, batting average and MES) to CricketX and obtain their respective CxBats as well as career ranks. It would objectively answer the question of whether the average Tendulkar was better than the average Jayasuriya. This is our first major step in evaluating the best batsman of all time. Why there is a second step is explained below but first—what are the career ranks yielded by CxBat?

According to Table 4.1, on a career average basis, the *best* ODI batsman is Vivian Richards with a CxBat index of 128. The second best ODI batsman is AB de Villiers, and Sachin Tendulkar is at 14, slightly ahead of Jayasuriya who is at 25. Also, note that in general, higher-ranked batsmen have a higher MES than lower-ranked batsmen, even in this tightly spaced list.

Table 4.1: Best Batsmen (Career Averages)

Rank	Batsman	Team	Conventional			Adjusted			CxBat
			SR	Avg	MES	SR	Avg	MES	
1	IVA Richards	WI	90.2	47.0	271	92.8	48.6	278	128
2	AB de Villiers	SA	96.0	51.5	288	83.5	47.8	250	121
3	MEK Hussey	AUS	87.2	48.2	262	83.4	46.5	250	120
4	Zaheer Abbas	PAK	84.8	47.6	254	82.5	46.8	248	120
5	GS Chappell	AUS	75.7	40.2	227	82.3	43.5	247	118
6	HM Amla	SA	88.3	53.2	265	78.1	48.6	234	117
7	L Klusener	SA	89.9	41.1	270	85.5	38.1	256	117
8	AC Gilchrist	AUS	96.9	35.9	287	88.8	33.5	266	116
9	A Symonds	AUS	92.4	39.8	277	85.1	36.3	255	115
10	MG Bevan	AUS	74.2	53.6	222	71.5	51.6	214	114
Special Mentions									
14	SR Tendulkar	IND	86.2	44.8	259	77.3	38.9	232	111
15	V Sehwag	IND	104.3	35.1	280	89.9	30.1	241	111
18	KP Pietersen	ENG	86.6	40.7	260	75.7	38.7	227	110
22	A Flintoff	ENG	88.8	32.0	256	84.2	30.3	243	109
25	ST Jayasuriya	SL	91.2	32.4	259	84.5	30.1	241	109

Source: CricketX database

Notes: 1. The batsmen are ranked by their CxBat (CricketX Batting Index) based on their career averages.

2. MES (Match Equivalent Score) = Minimum (SR * 3, Avg * 8)

3. The adjusted data is adjusted for pitch and opposition bowling strength.

We can call it a day here and declare our work done. But something does not feel right. The problem is this—how do you compare a Zaheer Abbas (62 innings) with Tendulkar (452 innings)? Even if one keeps a high minimum cut-off, say, 100 innings, there is still a problem with comparing someone like Klusener with Sachin Tendulkar based on their career averages when the former has played less than one-third the number of innings as the latter. If Klusener or Zaheer Abbas had played the same number of innings as Sachin or Jayasuriya had, would their career averages have been this high? Probably not.

So while CricketX has been able to provide us with rigorous answers to who is the best at any point in time, or whose career average is the best amongst all, it still has not answered who was the greatest of all batsmen. For greatness invokes a sense of time, rather of timelessness. We need to pin down this notion of greatness before we can expect CricketX to compute it for us.

Comparing and ranking greats is a familiar problem faced by analysts of all sports. Let us see if we can get some help from two sports where there is a 'reasonable' consensus on the greatest—tennis and golf. In tennis, Roger Federer is considered the greatest by many, even though he has not won a Grand Slam, i.e. won all four Grand Slam tournaments in the same year. On the other hand, Rod Laver has won a Grand Slam not once, but twice. So why is Federer considered the greatest? It is due in no small measure to the fact that he held the world No. 1 position for a record 302 weeks, including a 237-consecutive-week stretch from 2004 to 2008.

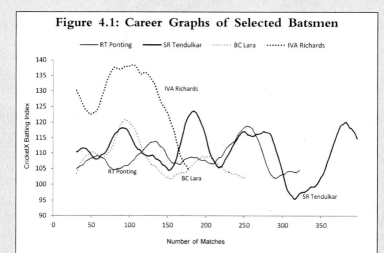

Figure 4.1: Career Graphs of Selected Batsmen

The chart tracks the four most-talked-about batsmen in ODI cricket—Richards, Tendulkar, Ponting and Lara.

The chart indicates where each batsman was with respect to others after the same number of matches in his career. For example, at the end of his 100th career match, Richards had by far the highest career average (in our terminology, the highest CxBat points). Lara's first peak coincides with Tendulkar's and so does Ponting's last. The Master Blaster had a long undulating career, and in his last stretch, post his 300th match, Tendulkar played like a young man again scoring around 1000 runs in his last twenty matches. Unfortunately, this comeback was not observed in his Test career.

S No.	Batsman	Team	Career	Inn	Runs	SR	Avg	CxBat	Career Avg Rank	Domi-nation Rank
1	IVA Richards	WI	1975–91	167	6721	90.2	47.0	128	1	1
2	SR Tendulkar	IND	1989–2012	452	18426	86.2	44.8	111	14	2
3	RT Ponting	AUS	1995–2012	365	13704	80.4	42.0	109	30	22
4	BC Lara	WI	1990–2007	289	10405	79.5	40.5	108	33	23

Source: CricketX database

In golf, the opinion almost universally is in favour of Tiger Woods even though he has fewer major victories (14) than another golfing legend, Jack Nicklaus (18). Why? Here is an answer from the popular website *about.com*:

> The height of Woods' accomplishments—both in terms of number of wins per year, in the way he dominated tournaments, in the way he dominated individual majors, in the multitude of monster seasons he's had, and the huge totals he's piled up in wins and majors—make him [the No. 1 in golf's all-time list].

There are similarities between the two respective greatest players and why they are considered to be the greatest. It is not about averages or transient peak performances or collecting all the trophies. It is about a sustained period of superlative performance, nay dominance. This is what we attempt to capture via our index of domination and longevity in our final reading of the data.

Measuring Longevity and Domination

In the previous chapter, while evaluating teams, we made similar distinctions between the best and the greatest. We tackled the problem of measuring longevity and domination by ranking all the teams by years and then looking at the teams which had been at the top the most number of times. We will do something similar here but on a bigger scale.

As discussed earlier, using the methodology outlined in this chapter, CricketX can tell us who the best players at any given point in time were (using their last thirty innings). So, that is what we asked CricketX to do. Starting from the inception of ODI cricket, at the end of each month, we ranked *all* the batsmen who were active then and not retired. Batsmen with less than thirty innings are not ranked. This yields a continuous monthly ranking of players (based on their last thirty innings) across the history of ODI cricket.

Now we do something that has not been done in this chapter until now and something that we are loathe to do—take a subjective call at how much importance to give to which rank. CricketX cannot do this for us. It is not a failure of CricketX or of statistics but it is our failure, because of not having a concrete definition of greatness. Given a definition, any definition, of greatness, CricketX can readily compute it for us, but in the absence of one, it won't be able to proceed. Computing the best at any given point is well defined—the player who will add the most to a team's strength at that particular time. Greatness over history is an even fuzzier concept.

After having conquered so much, we have been dealt a blow right at the end of our journey. This is the stuff Greek tragedies are made of. But, we will humour the gods and make a bold attempt. We compute a batsman's domination points by giving him three points for every month that he was ranked No. 1, two points if he was ranked No. 2 and one point if he was ranked No. 3. No points for any rank below No. 3. While these points are sensible but admittedly somewhat arbitrary, they will still reveal if we have a Federer or Woods equivalent amongst the batsmen in ODI cricket (Hint: We do!).

Here Comes the King

He swaggered in to bat. With ease, he dispatched all the bowlers to different parts of the cricket ground. When he got out, he swaggered back. A crumbling pitch did not matter, a fast-paced pitch was better. He was (is) brilliant, handsome, and his smile would charm the worst cynic. His name is Vivian Richards and he is the greatest one-day batsman in the world, ever.

If there is a phenomenon in one-day cricket that can attempt to match Don Bradman, it is Richards. Richards tops both the greatest and the best list. (As we will see in the next chapter on bowlers, it is not necessary that the best and the greatest is the same individual). In his career spanning seventeen years, Richards was the No. 1 batsman for fifty-one months and No. 2 for seventeen months. Adding up the weights for each rank (three for No. 1, two for No. 2 and one for No. 3) yields a domination points' aggregate of 188 for Richards. The domination of Vivian Richards is so complete that it offsets whatever subjectivity our points system might have introduced. Indeed, one can choose any sensible ranking and Richards comes out at the top. The second greatest all-time ODI batsman is the Master Blaster Sachin Tendulkar who, in a career span of 23 years, amassed 143 Domination Points.

Figure 4.2: Batsmen Domination

Source: CricketX database

Note: Months with ranks 1, 2 or 3 shaded for selected batsmen

Table 4.2: Greatest Batsmen

Rank	Batsman	Team	Career	Mat	Inn	Runs	No. of Months Ranked			Dom Points	Avg CxBat At Rank 1
							1	2	3		
1	IVA Richards	WI	1975–91	187	167	6721	51	17	1	188	134
2	SR Tendulkar	IND	1989–2012	463	452	18,426	20	29	25	143	123
3	AB de Villiers	SA	2005–	175	169	7210	31	16	5	130	131
4	A Symonds	AUS	1998–2009	198	161	5088	31	11	8	123	123
5	V Sehwag	IND	1999–2013	251	245	8273	25	6	10	97	127
6	A Flintoff	ENG	1999–2009	141	122	3394	21	11	0	85	126
7	ST Jayasuriya	SL	1989–2009	444	433	13,430	17	10	11	82	127
8	MEK Hussey	AUS	2004–12	185	157	5442	17	10	9	80	128
9	N Kapil Dev	IND	1978–94	225	198	3783	9	23	4	77	131
10	M Azharuddin	IND	1985–2000	334	308	9378	12	14	7	71	123
Special Mentions											
12	Saleem Malik	PAK	1982–99	283	256	7170	9	13	7	60	121
13	CH Lloyd	WI	1973–85	87	69	1977	10	7	7	51	127

13	ME Waugh	AUS	1988–2002	244	236	8500	14	4	1	51	122
17	AC Gilchrist	AUS	1996–2008	287	279	9619	3	7	25	48	120
18	L Klusener	SA	1996–2004	171	137	3576	13	0	4	43	138
19	HM Amla	SA	2008–	103	100	4946	0	12	16	40	
20	Javed Miandad	PAK	1975–96	233	218	7381	0	16	4	36	
31	RJ Hadlee	NZ	1973–90	115	98	1751	0	4	12	20	

Source: CricketX database

Notes: 1. The batsmen are ranked by their Domination Points.

2. Domination Points = (No. of Months Ranked 1) * 3 + (No. of Months Ranked 2) * 2 + No. of Months Ranked 3) * 1

3. Each month, batsmen are ranked on their batting index CxBat computed on the basis of their last 30 innings.

4. Average CxBat at Rank 1 is the average of the player's batting index CxBat when he was Rank 1.

There are some surprises. There are two contemporary players in the top twenty (both South Africans, both 30 years of age, and both with a few more years of cricket)—AB de Villiers (ranked 3) and Amla (ranked 19). De Villiers, with only thirteen domination points behind Tendulkar, looks set to surpass him. The other surprise is India's great all-rounder Kapil Dev. For three years, he was amongst the top three batsmen of his time.

'Batting for Vivian Richards is a matter of strokes, more strokes, and even more strokes.'
~John Arlott

'I saw him playing on television and was struck by his technique, so I asked my wife to come look at him. Now I never saw myself play, but I felt that this player is playing with a style similar to mine, and she looked at him on television and said yes, there is a similarity between the two...his compactness, technique, stroke production...it all seemed to gel!'
~Sir Donald Bradman on Sachin Tendulkar

The Present Best Batsmen

As promised earlier in the chapter, Table 4.3 presents our list of current best batsmen (as of 23 November 2014). The 'weight' of future batting lies on South Africa and India who occupy five slots each among the top twenty. Sri Lanka and Australia have three each, and New Zealand has two. Pakistan and West Indies each have only one batsman in the top twenty while England has none. If this list has hints about the World Cup, it is that South Africa is a strong contender for its maiden World Cup win. Australia (and New Zealand) will get a boost from the home advantage factor and this should make things interesting. Pakistan, England, New Zealand and West Indies however, would need a very strong bowling attack to have a chance at the World Cup. The next chapter discusses this, and much more.

Table 4.3: Best Batsmen—Present

Rank	Batsman	Team	Conventional			Adjusted (Last 30 Inn)			CxBat
			SR	Avg	MES	SR	Avg	MES	
1	AB de Villiers	SA	96.0	51.5	288	98.9	50.6	297	132
2	MS Dhoni	IND	89.3	52.9	268	80.8	55.6	242	122
3	V Kohli	IND	90.5	52.6	272	79.4	51.4	238	119
4	RA Jadeja	IND	84.6	34.5	254	81.1	44.4	243	117
5	AD Mathews	SL	85.6	40.9	257	75.6	50.2	227	116
6	KC Sangakkara	SL	77.5	40.0	233	80.6	39.6	242	114
7	HM Amla	SA	88.3	53.2	265	74.3	45.8	223	112
8	GJ Bailey	AUS	88.0	44.2	264	79.9	37.8	240	112
9	Misbah-ul-Haq	PAK	73.7	43.1	221	71.3	47.4	214	111
10	BB McCullum	NZ	90.6	30.1	240	86.2	31.3	250	111
11	JH Kallis	SA	72.9	44.4	219	76.1	40	228	111
12	Q de Kock	SA	88.4	43.6	265	80.7	34.3	242	110
13	RG Sharma	IND	81.0	37.9	243	73.3	42.9	220	110
14	DA Miller	SA	94.5	30.3	242	94.8	28.7	230	110
15	DJG Sammy	WI	101.3	23.7	189	94.8	28.4	227	109
16	TM Dilshan	SL	85.8	37.9	257	76.3	36.8	229	109

Rank	Batsman	Team	Conventional			Adjusted (Last 30 Inn)			CxBat
			SR	Avg	MES	SR	Avg	MES	
17	S Dhawan	IND	90.9	45.5	273	74.6	38.4	224	109
18	GJ Maxwell	AUS	120.4	29.7	238	109.6	24.7	198	107
19	JD Ryder	NZ	95.3	33.2	266	88.5	28.4	227	107
20	SPD Smith	AUS	87.7	31.8	254	83.6	29	232	107

Source: CricketX database

Notes: 1. The batsmen are ranked by their CxBat (CricketX Batting Index).

2. MES (Match Equivalent Score) = Minimum (SR * 3, Avg * 8)

3. The adjusted data is adjusted for pitch and opposition bowling strength.

Figure 4.3: Career Graphs of Selected Contemporary Batsmen

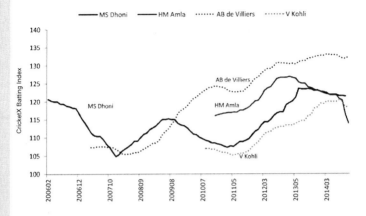

Source: CricketX database

The career path of four of the top ten contemporary batsmen—AB de Villiers, MS Dhoni, Virat Kohli, and Hashim Amla—is charted in Figure 4.3. This chart is across time, starting from the 30 innings for each batsman. The last point on the graph represents the present position of each batsman, as of end-November 2014. De Villiers has taken off like a rocket and is well ahead of the two Indian captains—Dhoni and Kohli—who seem to be in healthy competition with each other for the number two spot. Amla started out very well, reached a high peak of 125 CxBat at the end of 2012, but has since slipped considerably.

Batsman	Team	Career	Inn	Runs	SR	Avg	CxBat	Current Rank
AB de Villiers	SA	2005–	169	7210	96.0	51.5	132.3	1
MS Dhoni	IND	2004–	219	8192	89.3	52.9	122.1	2
V Kohli	IND	2008–	138	6208	90.5	52.6	119.1	3
HM Amla	SA	2008–	100	4946	88.3	53.2	112.4	9

Source: CricketX database

5

BOWLERS—UNSUNG HEROES

The bowler approached the wicket at a lope, a trot, and then a run. He suddenly exploded in a flurry of arms and legs, out of which flew a ball.

~Douglas Adams, *Life, the Universe and Everything*

There is evidence from pop sociology that among cricketers, the batsmen were the gentlemen, the real heroes. Schoolboys wanted their autographs, and schoolgirls drooled over them. The bowlers were just players who allowed the game to happen.

But cricket has come of age. Television brought the players home, especially after Kerry Packer introduced his innovations in the late 1980s. Dennis Lillee became the new macho man, and Imran Khan the new sex symbol. Both entertainers as well as superb fast bowlers. Toiling was suddenly being associated with greatness, and winning with hurling the ball at a speed approaching 90–95 mph. The genial Clive Lloyd recognized his heroes in Roberts, Holding, Garner and Marshall rather than in Greenidge, Haynes, Richards or himself. The new conquerors had arrived and it did not take long for schoolgirls and schoolboys to know who to look to for gazing and signatures. And then came the recognition that the prerogative of winning may lie more with the bowlers.

It used to be said that a leg-glance was one of the most elegant sights in cricket. Now it is a fast bowler's run-up—body bent slightly forward at first, then straightening as the momentum gathers, arms flailing about in a vertical freestyle action, the final jump, and bang—the ball delivered for the kill. All that for a split second of action, but what action!

Gone are the spinners, those practitioners of the gentle art of cricket. A tragedy—it is said that a true fast bowler does not give enough time for a batsman to make a mistake. And a spinner gives all the time in the world to make one.

But the spinners, though increasingly old hat in this fast-paced modern age, are beautiful in their action, in the wondrous flight they give the ball, and in the beauty by which the batsman is beaten. In sharp contrast to the fast bowler, the spinner's action is gentle, soothing, mesmerizing. As is their method of taking wickets. Spinners like to ensnare batsmen by employing a refined technique—some call it seduction. The ball is first hit for a six—round one to the batsman. The next ball is missed, and the battle won by the spinner.

'No cricketer is so dependent on the turf on which the game is played as the spinner; it can make, break, enfang or defang him.'

~Gideon Haigh

Both spinners and fast bowlers have been disadvantaged by advances in technology. The modern bowler does not find it any easier to spin the ball, though, at the margin, his better nutrition and fitness may allow him to bowl the ball faster than ever before. Clearly, there are many bowlers approaching a 100 mph speed, and certainly above 90 mph, on a consistent basis today. While rumoured to have touched 100 mph, neither Harold Larwood, nor Frank Tyson, nor Freddie Truman, are likely to have achieved that milestone. One might hastily conclude that there is balance in the bat–bowl world. But one couldn't be more wrong. Because batsmen in the present era, including ODI cricket, have a staggering amount of body protection which allows them to play the 95 mph speedsters with relative ease. There are arm pads, chest pads, helmets, enough to resemble a warrior in medieval times. And the bats today are so dense and have edges so thick that even a mis-hit reaches a boundary aided by the increased field restrictions.

The bowlers have tried hard to even the score. There has possibly been greater innovation in bowling than in batting. Yes, there is the helicopter shot, and the reverse sweep, which sometimes catches the fielders unawares, but these pale in comparison to the way bowlers have evolved in order to survive.

First, came the reverse swing, so complicated that one has to have knowledge of physics to explain it. This invention is attributed to Pakistani fast bowler Sarfraz Nawaz from the 1970s who taught it to Imran Khan, who in turn passed the secret on to Waqar Younis and Wasim Akram. The reverse swing is caused by a difference in the shine on the two sides of the ball. The rough side of the ball experiences more turbulence compared to the shiny side. Less air turbulence for the shiny side means less air resistance and hence the ball swings in that direction. For the batsman, the ball simply goes the other way.

It is meant to move in, but it swings out and you are caught in the slips. At other times, it swings in—when you thought it was going out—and either you are embarrassed from your stump flying off or, if you are lucky, you are out LBW.

Pakistan is also responsible for the other great innovation in bowling, the *doosra,* invented by one of the greatest spin bowlers of all time, Saqlain Mushtaq, in the 1990s. The *doosra,* which means 'the other one' or the second one', is an off-spinner's googly—a leg-break bowled with an off-break action. It was perfected by Muralitharan, who wielded it to amass 534 wickets over his career.

> '*Mate, if you just turn the bat over, you'll find instructions on the other side.*'
>
> ~Australian fast bowler Merv Hughes to Robin Smith after the England batsman repeatedly played and missed.

They Are All Contenders

Depending on one's choice of metaphor, the best and the greatest bowling field seems to be either congested or wide open. This is in stark contrast to the perception of the batting greats where there was almost complete certainty of who was number one and the interest in the rankings was, 'Who's (on) second?' For bowlers, there are claimants from all time periods for the number one spot—Ambrose, Garner, Imran Khan, McGrath and Pollock. Among the spinners, there are Muralitharan, Shane Warne and Saqlain Mushtaq. Can a choice be made? Can CricketX, armed with its regressions and correlations, pick the best and the greatest from the greats?

Symmetry with Batting

The game was given away in the previous chapter on batting—there is an overwhelming symmetry between the analysis of bowlers and batsmen. Instead of the strike rate for batsmen, there is the economy rate for bowlers—both are a measure of runs per ball scaled by a constant. And instead of batting average, runs per 'out' innings, there is the bowling average of runs given per wicket. And as in batting, we made adjustments for pitch and quality of bowling faced. Here, too, we make similar adjustments for pitch using the pitch index and for quality of batting faced using the CxBat of the opposition for every match.

Match Equivalent Score (MES) for Bowlers

Recall the MES of a batsman; it is analogously, and equivalently, defined for the bowler. Assume a hypothetical innings of just one bowler bowling for the entire innings, and the inning ends when, either fifty overs are bowled, or eight wickets are taken—whichever comes first. The MES is the minimum of the economy rate (defined as runs per ten overs) multiplied by five and the bowling average multiplied by eight (because there are on average eight outs in an ODI innings). Consider a bowler like Brett Lee whose career economy rate (runs per ten overs) is 47.6 and career bowling average (runs per wicket) is 23.4. If Lee bowled through the entire innings, the opposition score would be 187 runs. The economy rate side yields 238 runs but before the fifty overs are up, Lee would have 'bowled out' the opposition for 187 (23.4 * 8) runs.

Economy v Bowling Average

Apart from definitional parallels, there is empirical equivalence too. First, as with batting, the MES turns out to be the most important factor in determining the strength of a bowler and can indeed be used as a rough-and-ready reckoner for the more sophisticated CxBowl. MES is the best quick way to combine economy rate and bowling average.

Second, the (percentage) differences in economy rate are about twice as important as the (percentage) differences in bowling average—a similar result as obtained for batting. This is not at all to suggest that wicket-taking is not important. Rather, it is to assert that economizing on runs given is more critical in an ODI match where on average only eight wickets fall per innings. Looked at another way, misers win matches—where is Bapu Nadkarni when the game, and India, needs him!

One of the side effects of ODI on Test cricket is precisely the loss of bowlers like Bapu Nadkarni who exited before the advent of one-day cricket. He retired in 1967, and his record reads as follows:

Bowler	O	M	R	W	% Maidens
Bapu Nadkarni	1528	665	2559	88	44
Derek Underwood	3644	1239	7674	297	34

Note that Nadkarni was the number one maidens bowler—close to half his overs were maidens—and was far ahead of number two, Derek Underwood, who 'only' had one-third of his overs as maidens. In Test cricket, however, it is just the reverse—wickets taken count for much more than runs given away. They count for approximately twice than economy, i.e. a mirror image of ODIs.

> *'Nadkarni was famous for bowling an unerring line to batsmen which made it nearly impossible to score. It is often told that he used to put a coin on the pitch when he practiced in the nets, and would practice hitting the coin with every delivery.' (Wikipedia)*
> 'I tried to emulate Nadkarni in my youth; I hit the same spot only one out of six times.'
>
> ~Surjit S. Bhalla

The batting–bowling equivalence extends all the way to the construction of CxBowl and to the discussion of longevity and domination, measured in the same way. We ranked all the active bowlers each month since the beginning of ODI cricket, and then accorded bowling domination points—three points for rank one, two points for rank two and one point for rank three.

The Career Average Rankings

Table 5.1 lists the all-time top twenty best bowlers by their career averages. Occupying the No. 1 position is Big-Bird Joel Garner. Standing at an imposing 6 feet 8 inches, Garner was feared not only for his pace (no speed guns in the 1980s but he was fast) but also for his toe-crushing yorkers (think Malinga with an extra speed of 10 mph). He has the lowest economy rate of all—whether in conventional (31) or adjusted

(32.7) terms and his adjusted bowling average is 20.4—again one of the lowest.

The surprise entrant in the list, and occupying second position, is South Africa's LL Tsotsobe. His (adjusted) economy rate is a respectable 42.4 and his average is a superb 19.8. His CxBowl index, at 120, is only three points behind Joel Garner's. To be sure, he has not played as many matches as the others, but his talent is unmistakable. It is not clear why he was not part of the South Africa team that toured Australia in November 2014 and lost the series 4-1. It is likely, given his record, that the series would have been closer if he had been in the team. It remains to be seen whether he is included in the World Cup team, but clearly, CricketX recommends that he should be.

Shane Bond at No. 3 is yet another troubled talent. He is ahead of Brett Lee (ranked eleven) on both counts of adjusted economy and wicket-taking average. The rest of the top ten are made up of the usual suspects with only a couple of points to separate them. There are a number of disappointments, especially from Pakistan.

Both Tsotsobe and Shane Bond have a 'bad' economy rate yet emerge among the top three bowlers of all time. The reason is that they have an incredibly low adjusted bowling average—around 20 runs per wicket when most others are around 25, some 20–25 per cent higher!

Table 5.1: Best Bowlers (Career Averages)

Rank	Bowler	Team	Conventional				Adjusted			
			Econ	Avg	MES		Econ	Avg	MES	CxBowl
1	J Garner	WI	31.0	18.8	151		32.7	20.4	163	123
2	LL Tsotsobe	SA	47.5	25.0	200		42.4	19.8	158	120
3	SE Bond	NZ	42.9	20.9	167		41.2	20.4	163	119
4	SM Pollock	SA	36.8	24.5	184		34.8	23.5	174	116
5	AME Roberts	WI	34.1	20.4	163		35.6	22.1	177	116
6	CEL Ambrose	WI	34.8	24.1	174		34.8	25.4	174	116
7	DK Lillee	AUS	36.0	20.8	167		37.3	22.1	177	115
8	GD McGrath	AUS	38.8	22.0	176		37.2	22.3	178	115
9	MA Holding	WI	33.3	21.4	166		35.4	24.7	177	115
10	RJ Hadlee	NZ	33.4	21.6	167		36.7	25.1	184	112
Special Mentions										
11	B Lee	AUS	47.6	23.4	187		44.2	22.5	180	112
18	M Muralitharan	SL	39.3	23.1	185		38.2	25.3	191	110
24	WPUJC Vaas	SL	41.9	27.5	209		39.6	24.6	197	108

25	N Kapil Dev	IND	37.2	27.5	186	38.0	30.2	190	108
32	Wasim Akram	PAK	39.0	23.5	188	40.2	26.3	201	106
35	Imran Khan	PAK	39.0	26.6	195	39.9	28.4	199	106
38	A Flintoff	ENG	44.0	24.4	195	40.7	26.1	203	106
44	Saqlain Mushtaq	PAK	42.9	21.8	174	42.2	25.7	206	105
52	SK Warne	AUS	42.5	25.7	206	41.6	27.4	208	104
60	Waqar Younis	PAK	46.9	23.8	191	48.5	26.1	209	102

Source: CricketX database

Notes: 1. The bowlers are ranked by their CxBowl (CricketX Bowling Index).

2. MES (Match Equivalent Score) = Minimum (Econ * 5, Avg * 8)

3. The adjusted data is adjusted for pitch, opposition batting strength and quality of wickets taken.

MES for Bowlers:
Batting-Bowling Equivalence

$$\text{MES} = \text{Minimum of} \begin{cases} \text{Economy} * 50 \\ \text{Bowling Average} * 8 \end{cases}$$

Note:

Economy: Average number of runs given per over bowled

Bowling Average: Average number of runs given per wicket taken

The term MES is the same for a batsman and bowler. Why? Because of the *equivalence* between the economy rate of a bowler and the strike rate of a batsman; and the *equivalence* between the bowling average and the batting average. MES can also be thought of as the 'Mirror' Equivalent Score.

Figure 5.1: Career Graphs of Selected Bowlers

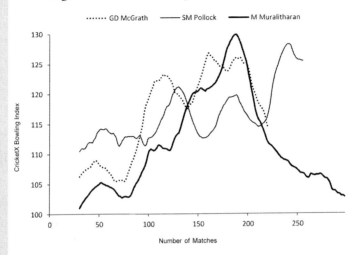

Source: CricketX database

The record of three of the greatest ODI bowlers—McGrath, Muralitharan and Pollock—indicates a near identical career path. By the strangest of co-incidences, all three reached a peak close to their respective 200th match. And then there is divergence—and what divergence for Pollock. The other two slide down and with Muralitharan experiencing a sharp, and longer, fall. In contrast, Pollock scaled newer, and greater, heights. At the time he retired, he was within inches of his peak CxBowl value of 127, and very close to Muralitharan's peak of 130.

S No.	Bowler	Team	Career	Mat	Runs	Wickets	Economy	Avg	Cx-Bowl	Career Avg Rank	Domination Rank
1	GD McGrath	AUS	1993–2007	248	8391	381	3.9	22.0	114.8	8	1
2	M Muralitharan	SL	1993–2011	341	12,326	534	3.9	23.1	109.8	18	3
3	SM Pollock	SA	1996–2008	297	9631	393	3.7	24.5	116.4	4	5

Source: CricketX database

Table 5.2: Greatest Bowlers

Rank	Bowler	Team	Career	Mat	Runs	Wickets	No. of Months Ranked 1	No. of Months Ranked 2	No. of Months Ranked 3	Domination Points	Avg CxBowl at Rank 1
1	GD McGrath	AUS	1993–2007	248	8391	381	39	36	9	198	130
2	CEL Ambrose	WI	1988–2000	175	5429	225	36	18	20	164	125
3	J Garner	WI	1977–87	98	2752	146	30	1	7	99	144
3	M Muralitharan	SL	1993–2011	341	12,326	534	17	20	8	99	130
5	SM Pollock	SA	1996–2008	297	9631	393	17	9	16	85	131
6	WPUJC Vaas	SL	1994–2008	320	11,014	400	11	15	17	80	129
7	RJ Hadlee	NZ	1973–90	112	3407	158	9	23	3	76	133
8	GF Lawson	AUS	1980–89	79	2592	88	14	9	15	75	123
8	AA Donald	SA	1991–2003	162	5926	272	9	18	12	75	125
10	SCJ Broad	ENG	2006–	108	4767	168	5	16	10	57	123
Special Mentions											
11	Waqar Younis	PAK	1989–2003	258	9919	416	15	2	4	53	127
16	Saqlain Mushtaq	PAK	1995–2003	165	6275	288	6	12	3	45	127
27	Imran Khan	PAK	1974–92	153	4844	182	0	6	5	17	
31	A Kumble	IND	1990–2007	265	10,412	337	2	2	3	13	122
42	SK Warne	AUS	1993–2003	191	7541	293	1	1	0	5	120
51	Wasim Akram	PAK	1984–2003	351	11,812	502	0	0	2	2	

Source: CricketX database

Notes: 1. The bowlers are ranked by their Domination Points.

2. Domination Points = (No. of Months Ranked 1) * 3 + (No. of Months Ranked 2) * 2 + (No. of Months Ranked 3) * 1

3. Each month, bowlers are ranked on their bowling index (CxBowl) computed on the basis of their last 30 innings.

4. Average CxBowl at Rank 1 is the average of the player's bowling index when he was ranked 1.

The Greatness Rankings

It is the Pigeon—McGrath! (Table 5.2). A card-carrying member of the greatest team to have played one-day cricket, Glenn McGrath was more than instrumental in making that achievement possible. Unlike batting, where Vivian Richards was at the top of both rankings, here the best ranking is different from the greatest ranking. Joel Garner, the best bowler, comes at No. 3 in the greatest bowlers; McGrath was ranked eighth in terms of career average.

The Garner and McGrath rankings bring into sharp focus the need to incorporate longevity in the calculation of the greatest. McGrath occupied the No. 1 rank 39 times and the No. 2 rank 36 times, both more than any other bowler ever. His bowling domination points are a whopping 198, *twice* those of Garner at 99.

Ambrose is the second greatest bowler with 164 points. McGrath and he form a separate class of their own. The others are far, far behind. Garner and Muralitharan are tied at the No. 3 spot with 99 points, a far cry from Ambrose's 164. Shaun Pollock follows with 85 points at No. 5. A slight surprise is the very high ranking received by the Sri Lankan Vaas, though his record suggests that this ranking is well deserved. His adjusted economy rate is 39.6 and his adjusted average is 24.6. He took 400 wickets, and was ranked the No. 1 bowler by CricketX eleven times.

Box 5.1: Shaun Pollock: Runs in the Family

'Considering the type of stuff floating around in his gene
pool, it would have been surprising if Shaun Pollock had
not been an international cricketer—and a very good one
at that. Dad Peter led the South African attack through
the 1960s; uncle Graeme was one of the finest, if not the
finest, left-hander to play the game. Shaun has bits of both
in his makeup, but it is as an immaculate, Hadlee-esque,
line and length seamer that he has established himself.'
Family in Cricket: Grandfather—AM Pollock; Great-
uncle—R Howden; Father—PM Pollock; Uncle—RG
Pollock; Cousin—AG Pollock; Cousin—GA Pollock.

—Peter Robinson/Jamie Alter *(ESPNcricinfo.com)*

Note the loneliness of the spinner in the list of the greatest.
Murali is the best spin bowler at No. 3, and Saqlain is the
next spinner (also an off-break bowler) at No. 16. But note
the wickets taken by Murali—534, the highest wicket-taker
in ODI history. Next on the highest wickets taken list is
Akram with 502 wickets—but ranked close to the bottom in
domination while Waqar Younis gets his due at No. 11—and
is the greatest Pakistani bowler.

No matter how one slices the data—conventional averages,
adjusted averages, match equivalent scores or domination
points—the spinners, barring a couple, are like the invisible
hand, nowhere to be seen. Pace bowling pays more; more
wickets, and a better economy rate. Out of the top twenty
bowlers, only two are spinners; out of the top forty, only six
are spinners.

Shane Warne ranks low in both ODI career average ranking (No. 52) and the domination ranking (No. 42). Before we began this quest, we thought that the Murali–Warne comparison would be an epic fight for supremacy, a fight whose analysis would define, and refine, our method of evaluating and ranking players. This debate has raged for many years—who is the better bowler, Shane or Murali? It wasn't helped by the fact that Murali was called for his action by the umpires, and the cricketing authorities. He was eventually cleared but it left a bad taste. However, going by the numbers, there is just no contest. Shane, the ODI player is less than a shadow of Shane, the Test player; and less than a shadow of Murali in ODIs.

'I just try to bore the batsmen out. It's pretty simple stuff but the complicated thing is to keep it simple.'

~Glenn McGrath

'He demolished batting line-ups when it mattered.'

~Allan Donald on Curtly Ambrose

'They should cut Joel Garner off at the knees to make him bowl at a normal height.'

~Geoffrey Boycott

'He turns round to Kaluwitharana and asks him what I'm bowling. Kalu says offspin. Border hits the next one, but he's not confident. He asks Dean Jones, the non-striker, what I'm doing, and he says legbreaks.'

~Muttiah Muralitharan recalls Allan Border's reaction on facing him for the first time, in 1992

Figure 5.2: Bowlers Domination

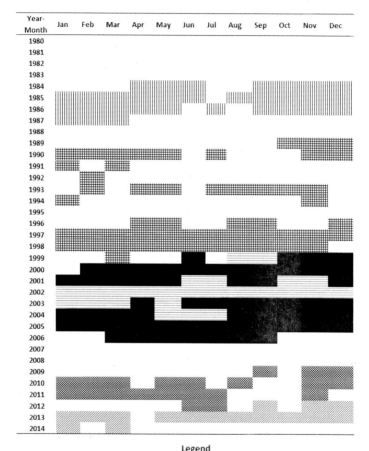

Legend

Bowler	Dom. Rank	Bowler	Dom. Rank
GD McGrath	1	M Muralitharan	4
CEL Ambrose	2	SCJ Broad	10
J Garner	3	Saeed Ajmal	17

Source: CricketX database

Note: Months with Ranks 1 or 2 shaded for selected bowlers.

The Present Best

Table 5.3 lists the best among contemporary bowlers. Topping this list are two English bowlers—James Anderson and Steven Finn. Next is Pakistan's Saeed Ajmal, another bowler whose action has been questioned. Is this another Murali story or does he genuinely have a problem? And is it in the nature of competition that very successful off-spinners are questioned for their action or is it the other way around, i.e. that a questionable action makes the bowlers better?

In the contemporary list for batsmen, it was noted that England, Pakistan, West Indies and New Zealand had a meagre presence in the list of the best. This imbalance is being partly redressed—Pakistan has two bowlers in the top ten itself, Sri Lanka has three in the top twenty, and West Indies has three as well (Rampaul, Narine and Taylor). India also has two bowlers, Ravichandran Ashwin and Mohammad Shami. This current best list suggests a closer World Cup than that indicated by the batting list. However, batting and bowling lists taken together suggest that Australia and South Africa are still the teams to beat, especially with Australia playing at home.

Table 5.3: Best Bowlers—Present

Rank	Bowler	Team	Conventional			Adjusted			CxBowl
			Econ	Avg	MES	Econ	Avg	MES	
1	JM Anderson	ENG	49.4	29.1	233	38.7	19.7	158	121
2	ST Finn	ENG	47.5	28.4	227	39.2	21.9	175	115
3	Saeed Ajmal	PAK	41.4	22.2	177	40.8	22.4	179	113
4	DW Steyn	SA	48.3	25.7	205	39.4	22.8	183	112

Rank	Bowler	Team	Conventional			Adjusted			CxBowl
			Econ	Avg	MES	Econ	Avg	MES	
5	DL Vettori	NZ	41.2	31.8	206	37.5	26.6	187	110
6	Junaid Khan	PAK	51.4	25.9	207	47.7	22.7	182	110
7	MG Johnson	AUS	48.3	25.7	206	41.9	24.0	192	108
8	R Rampaul	WI	50.8	29.2	234	47.6	23.8	190	107
9	R Ashwin	IND	49.0	32.5	245	40.5	26.4	202	105
10	AD Mathews	SL	45.6	35.7	228	38.4	35.6	192	105
11	JE Taylor	WI	48.8	27.3	218	43.7	25.3	202	105
12	CJ McKay	AUS	47.8	24.4	195	42.6	25.6	204	104
13	SP Narine	WI	41.1	26.5	205	40.6	28.1	203	104
14	Mohammed Shami	IND	57.5	26.1	209	49.9	25.0	200	103
15	R McLaren	SA	52.5	27.3	218	49.5	25.2	202	103
16	M Morkel	SA	49.4	24.3	194	45.4	25.8	206	103
17	BAW Mendis	SL	45.9	20.8	166	46.8	25.6	205	103
18	TG Southee	NZ	51.8	31.7	253	46.1	25.8	206	103
19	KD Mills	NZ	47.3	26.8	215	43.1	27.0	216	101
20	TM Dilshan	SL	47.8	47.4	239	39.6	44.4	198	101

Source: CricketX database

Notes: 1. The bowlers are ranked by their CxBowl (CricketX Bowling Index) .

2. MES (Match Equivalent Score) = Minimum (Econ * 5, Avg * 8)

3. The adjusted data is adjusted for pitch, opposition batting strength and quality of wickets taken.

Figure 5.3: Career Graphs of Selected Contemporary Bowlers

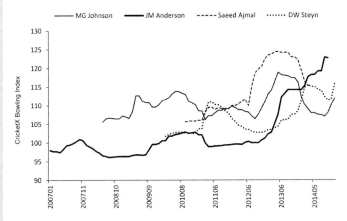

Source: CricketX database

Saeed Ajmal is going to be missed in World Cup 2015 because of investigation for his bowling action. Look at his record. A steep climb to his peak and then a gradual decline—and then a full stop because of his action being called. The bowler to watch in the World Cup is none other than the presently ranked No. 1 bowler, Jim Anderson. He was an average good bowler in the first two-thirds of his career—and then he takes off, and actually outperforms every other bowler—including himself, and the absent Ajmal. The other bowler to note is Dale Steyn—his graph suggests that he might be *the* challenger to Anderson in the months ahead. And don't forget Mitchell Johnson playing on home turf.

S No.	Bowler	Team	Career	Mat	Runs	Wickets	Econ	Avg	Cx-Bowl	Current Rank
1	JM Anderson	ENG	2002–	181	7480	257	4.94	29.1	121.3	1
2	Saeed Ajmal	PAK	2008–	110	4059	183	4.14	22.2	112.7	3
3	DW Steyn	SA	2006–	92	3720	145	4.83	25.7	112.0	4
4	MG Johnson	AUS	2005–	141	5685	221	4.83	25.7	108.3	7

Source: CricketX database

6

ALL–ROUNDERS—DOWN WITH
SPECIALIZATION

A human being should be able to change a diaper, plan an
invasion, butcher a hog, conn a ship, design a building, write
a sonnet, balance accounts, build a wall, set a bone, comfort
the dying, take orders, give orders, cooperate, act alone, solve
equations, analyse a new problem, pitch manure, program a
computer, cook a tasty meal, fight efficiently, die gallantly.
Specialization is for insects.

~Robert A. Heinlein

It is (unfairly) said of Gerry Ford, the thirty-eighth President
of the US, that he could not walk and chew gum at the
same time. In cricket, there is one individual who revels in
walking, eating gum, and in being in two places at the same
time—the all-rounder. A person who can both bat and bowl;
actually, that should read bat, bowl *or* wicket-keep. But then
there are the interlopers, the fast bowlers who by intimidating
the batsmen have found that they would like to be on the
receiving end, presumably to show the established batsmen
how the bowling should be handled. In the post-War period,
this set of Test all-rounders reads like a who's who of fast

bowlers—Ray Lindwall, Alan Davidson, Imran Khan, Richard Hadlee, Kapil Dev and even Malcolm Marshall.

Given the symmetry between batsman and bowler statistics, it is a simple matter to define the all-rounder score as some combination of the bowling and batting indices (CxBat and CxBowl) for identifying the best and the batting and bowling domination points for calculation of the greatest. However, bear in mind that we are raising the bar very high when we judge all-rounders by the extent to which they have dominated the specialized areas of batting and bowling separately. Only the greatest of greats will pass through.

All-rounder Rankings—The Best

Before we evaluate all-rounders, we need to define the term. We want to look at the combination of batting and bowling strengths but we also want to demand a minimum for both, otherwise players exceptional in one discipline like Richards and Tendulkar will come out ahead on the basis of their batting alone. In fact, building on the same insight, we offer the following metric for ranking all-rounders: the minimum of his batting and bowling skills. The maximum of the two skills represents heights of specialization, while the minimum emphasizes breadth, the true mark of an all-rounder.

There are less than ten players who can boast of having both their batting and bowling *career averages* above par (i.e. above 100). This shows just how *incredibly* difficult it is to achieve this over one's entire career. The table below shows the list of top ten all-rounders. The All-rounder Index, CxAR, in the table below is the minimum of a player's CxBat and CxBowl.

Table 6.1: All-rounders—Masters of Two Trades

Rank	Player	Team	CxBat	CxBowl	CxAR
1	N Kapil Dev	IND	108	108	108
2	Imran Khan	PAK	108	106	106
3	A Flintoff	ENG	109	106	106
4	AD Mathews	SL	109	104	104
5	CL Hooper	WI	106	102	102
6	RA Jadeja	IND	105	102	102
7	SM Pollock	SA	101	116	101
8	SP O'Donnell	AUS	104	100	100
9	JR Hopes	AUS	101	100	100
10	SR Watson	AUS	107	100	100

Source: CricketX database

It is a clash between the icons of the two biggest cricket playing nations. Kapil Dev emerges ahead as the best all-rounder with a beautiful balance between the bat and the ball, capturing the very essence of the word all-rounder (a good validation of our definition). He was voted as India's Cricketer of the Century by Wisden in 2002, ahead of Sunil Gavaskar and Sachin Tendulkar. Not a bad choice at all!

As for Imran Khan, the Pakistani heart-throb, journalist Martin Williamson writes:

Thousands, if not millions, who had never dreamt of bowling fast on heartless baked mud suddenly wanted to emulate Imran and his lithe bounding run, his leap and his reverse-swinging yorker. He also made himself into an all-rounder worth a place for his batting alone, and captained Pakistan as well as anyone, rounding off his career with the 1992 World Cup.

Andrew Flintoff is close at his heels at No. 3. A tall (6 feet 4 inches) fast bowler, batsman and slip fielder, Flintoff was consistently rated by the ICC as being among the top international all-rounders in both ODI and Test cricket (Wikipedia). He had retired from active cricket in 2009 due to a devastating knee injury, but is planning a comeback. A true all-rounder—during his retirement, he even tried his hand at professional boxing, winning the first and only match he took part in.

Amongst the new crop, Angelo Mathews leads the brigade and is a prized possession of the Sri Lanka team. In February 2013, he became Sri Lanka's youngest ever Test captain at the age of 25.

> 'In baseball, my theory is to strive for consistency, not to worry about the numbers. If you dwell on statistics you get short-sighted, if you aim for consistency, the numbers will be there at the end.'
>
> ~Tom Seaver

Enough of the best. What about the greatest?

The Greatest All-rounders—The Famous Quartet of the 1980s

The 1980s was a fascinating decade with a quartet of all-rounders competing for greatness—Richard Hadlee (NZ), Ian Botham (ENG), Imran Khan (PAK) and Kapil Dev (IND). Talking about the rivalry between the four, Hadlee said in an interview in 2013: 'I didn't want to get out to Kapil or

Immy (Imran) or Beefy (Botham) but I certainly wanted to get them out when I bowled. So that competition actually grew and that motivation actually grew.'

On the question of the best, Hadlee replied: 'If I was asked to pick who was the better of the four of us, and I am on record as saying Imran because he was a versatile batsman, potent strike bowler and charismatic captain.' Remember in those days, majority of the cricket played was Test cricket and players were judged by fans and each other on the basis of their Test performances. What about the quartet's ODI exploits—has their dominance been upended?

There are only eight players in CricketX database who have at least one domination point in both batting and bowling—we warned you that this was going to be a high bar. The entire list is presented in the table below, ranked by the minimum of the two domination points. Even after almost twenty-five years, the quartet still towers over the others, occupying four of the top six places, and as for the greatest amongst them, it is not Imran Khan, Sir Richard Hadlee. It is you.

Table 6.2: All-rounder Domination: The Quartet Still Rules

Rank	Player	Domination Points			
		Batting	Bowling	Total	Min
1	RJ Hadlee	20	76	96	20
2	N Kapil Dev	77	4	81	4
2	SR Watson	4	16	20	4
3	Imran Khan	3	17	20	3
3	JDP Oram	8	3	11	3
3	IT Botham	5	3	8	3
3	Shakib Al Hasan	4	3	7	3
4	A Flintoff	85	1	86	1

Source: CricketX database

Note: Players have been ranked on the minimum of the two domination points—batting and bowling.

Wicketkeepers

Conventionally, an all-rounder is someone who can both bat and bowl. This convention was weakened when Jonty Rhodes of South Africa exploded on to the fielding scene. Suddenly, saving runs was just as important as scoring runs, and a player who could both field and bat, well, he was marginally preferable to one whose mixture of batting and bowling was not of the greatest value. This also coincided with (and we speculate, was a result of) the declining importance of bowling.

But what about those who stand and serve behind the stumps? Unlike baseball, some of the greatest batsmen in ODI cricket are the catchers i.e. the wicketkeepers. The wicketkeepers are the new all-rounders. Just look at the 'monopolized' list of wicketkeepers today; each wicketkeeper plays for a long, long time. Simultaneously, look at the list of the best (or greatest) batsmen. There is a good degree of agreement! Adam Gilchrist, who recently retired from Test and ODI cricket, played 287 matches, has a career rank of 8 and a domination rank of 17. Sangakkara of Sri Lanka is a veteran of 382 matches, and has a career rank of 56 owing to a less illustrious start. Today he ranks at No. 7. India's MS Dhoni has played in 250 matches, and he has a career rank of 11 and a current rank of 2. Such distinguished records demand that we also analyse wicketkeepers in order to identify the best all-rounder.

Unfortunately, there no simple way to compare the wicketkeeper's contribution to that of the bowler, and this remains a future area of work for CricketX. Table 6.3 presents the most successful wicketkeepers of ODI cricket. Adam

Gilchrist, Kumar Sangakkara and MS Dhoni are three of the top four wicketkeepers of all time! They just might turn out to be the best and greatest all-rounders of ODI cricket.

Table 6.3: Wicketkeepers with Most Dismissals

Rank	Player	Team	Career	Mat	Catches	Stump	Dismissals
1	AC Gilchrist	AUS	1996–2008	287	417	55	472
2	KC Sangakkara	SL	2000–	385	361	92	453
3	MV Boucher	SA	1998–2011	295	402	22	424
4	MS Dhoni	IND	2004–	250	227	85	312
5	Moin Khan	PAK	1990–2004	219	214	73	287
6	BB McCullum	NZ	2002–	232	227	15	242
7	IA Healy	AUS	1988–97	168	194	39	233
8	Rashid Latif	PAK	1992–2003	166	182	38	220
9	RS Kaluwitharana	SL	1990–2004	189	131	75	206
10	PJL Dujon	WI	1981–91	169	183	21	204

Source: CricketX database

7

THE ART AND SCIENCE OF CAPTAINCY

My responsibility is getting all my players playing for the name on the front of the jersey, not the one on the back.

~Unknown

When director Sam Mendes was having problems with his first film crew on the sets of *American Beauty*, the book he reached for advice was Mike Brearley's *The Art of Captaincy*. Brearley, considered one of the greatest captains ever and indeed judged to be the best in BTW (1987), was said to have a 'degree in people'. People management is what a captain needs to get the best out of his players—as exemplified by Imran Khan and his Pakistani team of the late 1980s and early 1990s. Pakistan did win the World Cup in Australia in 1992, a victory in no small measure due to the band of talented *individual* Pakistani players, and to Imran's ability to make them perform better than they would otherwise.

However, good people skills alone do not make a good captain in cricket. Cricket captains, unlike those in most other sports, are required to take all the tactical decisions on the field and are thus integral to the success of a team. As Brearley himself put it in an interview, 'Technically, you need to know the game completely. You need to have a great pleasure and interest in tactics. You need to be both inventive and cautious, and move between attack and defense without too much of a radical shift.'

How do we measure the contribution of captaincy? The traditional way, of looking at just the win record of a captain to evaluate him, is flawed, because it does not take into account how good the team was by itself. Good captaincy should result in a team winning more matches *than it would have otherwise*—or in other words, perform better than *expected*, given its ability. Hence, it is not about performance but outperformance. But that just deflects the problem, doesn't it? No, it does not, not with CricketX at our disposal.

As outlined in Chapter 2, the entire superstructure of our analysis, and inferences, is based on measuring expectations and tallying them with actual results. Specifically, for every match, CricketX computes a *prior* probability of the teams winning or losing the match based on their respective team strengths. This is what CricketX expects from the two teams given their stats. Whether they did better or worse can now easily be evaluated against this statistical expectation. Before we look at the individual records of captains, let us examine the overall out/underperformance record of the teams in ODI cricket. Which do you think is the most underperforming team in ODI history?

Box 7.1: Brearley's Degree in People

Here is an example told by Bob Willis, a fast bowler in Brearley's side. Willis was involved in Brearley's occasional winding up of the swashbuckling Ian Botham. When he felt that he needed to ginger Botham up, Brearley would signal to Willis, to take a message to Botham: 'Mike says that you're bowling like a girl.' Pity the poor batsman who faced the next ball from a seething Botham. Willis concluded this by saying that if the captain had used the same words with him, it would have destroyed his confidence and had the opposite effect. Useful things, degrees in people.

Teams: Achievements v Expectations

Everybody's *favourite* 'underperforming' team is South Africa. As documented in Table 7.1, in reality, it turns out that South Africa is the best performer relative to expectations, or more accurately, pre-match expectations (what transpires in the match is analysed in the next chapter on stress). According to the CricketX model, they should have won 54 per cent of their matches; they won 59 per cent—a good 5 per cent outperformance across history. The second best performer is Australia with 4 per cent extra wins. And the wooden spoon goes to—New Zealand, which has lost 4 per cent more matches than it should have. Sri Lanka's underperformance was mostly before the 1990s and England has been the worst underperformer since then, followed by New Zealand and West Indies.

Table 7.1: Team Performance Relative to Expectations across ODI History

Team	Expected Win %	Actual Win %	Extra Win %	Extra Win % since 1990
AUS	57	61	4	6
ENG	48	45	-3	-6
IND	49	48	-1	1
SL	46	43	-3	0
NZ	46	42	-4	-5
PAK	48	49	1	1
SA	54	59	5	5
WI	49	50	1	-4
Total	50	50	0	0

Source: CricketX database

Notes: 1. This table only includes the ODI matches between the eight teams amongst themselves.

2. The Expected Win % has been computed using the CricketX model.

3. Extra Win % = Actual Win % − Expected Win %

Figure 7.1 graphs the actual v the expected performance of teams across ODI history with a dashed line separating the outperformers, those above the line or the A-students, from the underachievers; those below the line are the C-students.

Figure 7.1: Team Performance Relative to Expectations across ODI History

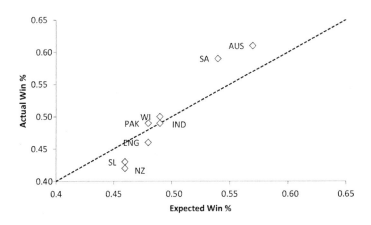

Source: CricketX database

Measuring Captaincy

To be sure, better or worse than expected is a function of various causes and before using it as an indicator to measure captaincy, we need to delve deeper. A team can outperform over time for essentially two reasons—the same players start playing better, and/or there is an influx of new and better players. The former squarely falls in our definition of what a good captain must achieve. So does the latter, for the captain is an important voice in squad selection and decides the playing eleven.

We can now progress to answering the original question of who is the greatest captain in ODI history. It deserves emphasis that CricketX's method of evaluation relies not on the *level* of performance, but on the *level* of outperformance. Therefore, the method does not penalize a good captain for a bad inheritance, or reward a bad one for performing only in line with the team's capabilities.

The Best and the Greatest

For every captain, we look at his expected and his achieved win record, the gap between the two being our proxy for measuring captaincy. As in the previous chapters, here too we encounter the issue of the best v the greatest but fortunately, the resolution is quite straightforward. We use Extra Wins percentage as our measure of efficiency of his captaincy (value added per match or 'best-ness') and we incorporate longevity by calculating the *actual* number of Extra Wins (Actual Wins–Expected Wins) earned by the captain over his captaincy career. By definition,

Extra Wins = Actual Wins − Expected Wins
*= Number of Matches as Captain * Extra Win %*

As a side and somewhat obvious note, while ranking the best captains, we need to use some minimum cut-off, say 30, for the number of matches captained to get useful results. Otherwise, Shane Warne of Australia, who has won 10 out of the 11 matches he has captained, will easily trump all the captains with a longer captaincy career. He will, in turn, be trumped by the likes of Geoff Boycott who won both the matches he captained. Note, however, that no such cut-off is needed while ranking players for greatness using Extra Wins, since it already incorporates longevity.

Table 7.2 lists both the best and the greatest captains in one-day cricket. Since there is a lot of overlap between the two lists, they have been presented in the same table. The table, however, is ranked by greatness, i.e. Extra Wins—a measure that we think befits our goal better. The three 'best' ranked captains not in the greatest ten have been listed as special mentions and the actual 'best' ranking can be deduced by looking at the Extra Win percentage.

Table 7.2: The Best and the Greatest Captains in ODI Cricket

Rank	Captain	Team	Career	Mat	Expected Win %	Actual Win %	Extra Win %	Extra Wins
1	WJ Cronje	SA	1994–2000	125	59.7	72.4	12.7	15.9
2	CH Lloyd	WI	1975–85	80	61.8	78.1	16.3	13.1
3	RT Ponting	AUS	2002–12	189	68.0	74.6	6.6	12.4
4	MS Dhoni	IND	2007–	137	53.3	61.7	8.3	11.4
5	Imran Khan	PAK	1982–92	131	49.5	56.9	7.4	9.7
6	Wasim Akram	PAK	1993–2000	103	51.4	60.2	8.8	9.1
7	AR Border	AUS	1985–94	169	56.7	61.8	5.2	8.8
8	MW Gatting	ENG	1986–88	36	50.8	69.4	18.7	6.7

Rank	Captain	Team	Career	Mat	Expected Win %	Actual Win %	Extra Win %	Extra Wins
9	GC Smith	SA	2003–11	128	57.2	62.1	4.9	6.2
10	SR Waugh	AUS	1997–2002	99	58.0	64.1	6.1	6.0
Special Mentions								
11	Shoaib Malik	PAK	2007–09	33	47.0	63.6	16.6	5.5
14	MS Atapattu	SL	2001–06	59	49.1	57.6	8.5	5.0
15	MJ Clarke	AUS	2008–	58	59.9	67.2	7.4	4.3

Source: CricketX database

Notes: 1. The captains are ranked on Extra Wins—our measure of greatness.
2. Expected Win % is computed using the CricketX model and is based on the team strength.
3. Extra Win % = Actual Win % − Expected Win %.
4. Extra Wins = Number of Matches Captained * Extra Win %
5. Only matches amongst the 10 ICC full-member teams have been considered. Also, some matches have been excluded for data issues.

Do Captains Make Match-Winning Decisions after Winning the Toss?

% Matches won when:

Lost Toss	Won Toss	Toss Adv %
49.9	50.1	0.2

% Matches won when batting:

First	Second	Chasing Adv %
49.0	51.0	2.0

Source: CricketX Database

**Winning the toss does not matter!
Batting second helps.**

Who Is the Greatest Captain in All ODI History?

It is Hansie Cronje of South Africa, who earned 16 more victories for South Africa by virtue of his captaincy. Clive Lloyd is second with 13 Extra Wins from two-thirds as many matches (80 v Cronje's 125). Let us look at that best v greatest distinction again. One might make the claim that Lloyd should be number one, because his Extra Win percentage is larger than that of Cronje. Lloyd won 16.3 per cent more matches, compared to Cronje's 12.7 per cent. Why not Mike Gatting then, who won 18.7 per cent more matches? In fact, Gatting is a perfect example to illustrate the difference between being the best and being the greatest.

He [Gatting] captained England to an Ashes series victory in Australia in 1986/87. In 1987, Gatting gained notoriety in the 'Shakoor Rana affair' when he argued with umpire Shakoor Rana in Faisalabad. He was accused of adjusting the field illegally, i.e. after the bowler had started running in, and warned... An argument ensued, during the course of which Rana accused Gatting of breaking the rules and Gatting shouted 'We made the rules.' He had to be dragged away. Martin Williamson, editor of *Cricinfo*, subsequently commented of the incident, 'Whatever the provocation, Gatting was in the wrong.' Gatting also reflected later that 'it wasn't a very proud moment of my career'. He also admitted that, whatever the official reason given, it was the real reason why he lost the England captaincy the following summer.

(Wikipedia)

Longevity is a virtue that one deserves no small credit for. Think of it this way—if Cronje, or for that matter Ponting, kept the job longer than others, it was because they met the stringent requirements for longer; hence, Cronje and Ponting should get credit for extra wins derived from longevity.

As it turns out, there is more to the Cronje story, or more accurately, saga. He was found guilty of the crime of match-fixing. However, note the irony—you can only fix to lose or do worse, and hence it can only *depress* your record as a captain. Here, Cronje is consistently winning 13 per cent *more* matches. So, he is unlikely to have been a congenital match-fixer. However, spot-fixing is entirely within the realm of winning 'extra' matches and fixing a few spots along the way.

There is an interesting coincidence between the Test and the ODIs regarding the result about captaincy. As mentioned at the start of this chapter, BTW (1987) had a (non-conventional) finding as the best Test captain—the psychologist gentleman captain of England, Mike Brearley. As everyone knows, Brearley contributed very little with the bat in Test cricket. Indeed, BTW did not even rank him in the top 105 Test batsmen. Cronje averages a healthy 37 runs in ODI but with a very low strike rate of 73, his overall rank as an ODI batsman is a low 80.

Another interesting observation is that while the Waugh–Ponting Australian team of 2000s pips the Lloyd/Richards West Indies team of the 1970s–80s for the greatest ever, Clive Lloyd himself is a shade ahead of Ponting, even if barely so. It is worth mentioning that even if one uses the conventional stats of actual win percentage, Lloyd, Ponting and Cronje make the top three, all of them above a phenomenal 70 per cent. And

Cronje obviously had the *least* strongest of the three teams to lead. So, it is not a surprise that he turns out to be the greatest captain in our analysis.

MS Dhoni of India, the only currently playing captain in the top ten, is ranked high at No. 4 and is within striking distance of Ponting. Imran Khan, No. 5, is undoubtedly the greatest captain Pakistan had. Steve Waugh is ranked No. 10—thus, that other debate—who was a better captain, Ricky or Steve—seems to be settled in favour of Ponting. However, do note the close correspondence in the Extra Win percentage—6.6 per cent for Ponting and 6.1 per cent for Steve Waugh. Close but with an advantage to Ponting. And over all the matches that Ponting captained, he provided twelve extra wins to Australia versus only six for Steve Waugh.

Two other 'intriguing' findings. First, that barring Zimbabwe and Bangladesh, England has three of the nine worst captains in ODI history. This is entirely consistent with our findings at the team level—England, on average, had a 3 per cent lower winning rate than they should have and one which worsened after 1990.

The second interesting finding is that the second greatest batsman in ODI history, Sachin Tendulkar, has one of the worst records amongst all captains—an Extra Loss percentage of 12 and 7.2 Extra Losses over his captaincy career. We can now truly understand his agony when he writes of 1997:

> However, things were really starting to get on top of me. I hated losing and as captain of the team I felt responsible for the string of miserable performances. More worryingly, I did not know how I could turn it around, as I was

already trying my absolute best... Losing a string of very close matches had left me badly scarred... The fact that we failed to chase down 120 had *nothing to do with lack of talent.* (emphasis added)

(After the Barbados defeat, Sachin Tendulkar considered quitting cricket, *Indian Express*, 3 November 2014.)

'*Nothing to do with lack of talent.*' Well, at least Sachin was never in denial. It is remarkable how good our indicator has turned out to be in uncovering good and bad captaincy, even though it took some faith in applying it.

Box 7.2: Does Winning the Toss Matter?

There is an old saying about winning the toss in Test cricket. Think hard and deep about fielding—and then decide to bat. In ODIs, commentators have at times proclaimed—win the toss, win the match. So do captains make match-winning decisions after winning the toss?

Table 7.3: Does Winning the Toss Matter? Or Batting Second?

Team	% Matches Won			% Matches Won Batting		
	Lost Toss	Won Toss	Toss Adv %	First	Second	Chasing Adv %
AUS	62.5	60.4	-2.1	61.9	60.8	-1.1
ENG	44.3	47.2	2.9	39.5	51.8	12.3
IND	47.1	50.1	3.0	45.1	52.0	6.9
SL	43.5	42.3	-1.2	43.6	42.2	-1.4
NZ	43.7	40.2	-3.5	39.2	44.8	5.6

Team	% Matches Won			% Matches Won Batting		
	Lost Toss	Won Toss	Toss Adv %	First	Second	Chasing Adv %
PAK	49.6	48.2	-1.4	50.7	46.8	-3.9
SA	57.1	61.1	4.0	59.1	59.2	0.1
WI	50.0	50.6	0.6	49.6	50.8	1.2
Total	49.9	50.1	0.2	49.0	51.0	2.0

Source: CricketX Database

Winning the Toss Does Not Matter!

The captains might as well toss a coin to decide who goes first. On average, winning the toss has not led to any significant increase in percentage of matches won (49.9 % v 50.1%). The only notable exceptions are South Africa, and to some extent India and England, who seemed to have extracted some benefit from it.

Batting Second Helps

On average, teams win 2 per cent more matches while chasing than while setting the target. English teams have won an extra 12 per cent of their matches when they chose to bat second or when their opponents did them a favour by batting first. India and New Zealand also turn out to be good chasers while Pakistan has had more luck while defending their score. The other major teams are really indifferent to batting first or second.

8

UPSETS, COMEBACKS AND THE STRESS IN BETWEEN

*If you can keep your head when all about you are losing
theirs and blaming it on you...'*

~Rudyard Kipling, 'If'

*To dream the impossible dream
To fight the unbeatable foe
To bear with unbearable sorrow
To run where the brave dare not go*

~'The Impossible Dream', from *Man of La Mancha*

Ah, the magnificent uncertainties of cricket. This chapter is
devoted to identifying the most formidable situations of ODI
cricket and analysing how individuals and teams play under
stress. Keep calm and carry on is good advice for a poster, but
in the nervous moments of duress, there are goof-ups, there
are easy catches dropped by butterfingers (possibly caused by
the sweat due to stress!) and there are loose cannons instead of
straight deliveries. Mind you, the players selected for an ODI,

or for that matter any other sport at the international level, have already passed through several tests of their expertise to play under pressure.

Forget cricket—try taking an exam, or for that matter playing the stock market—stress management separates the winners from the losers. What statistics can unravel the mystery of stress—who plays the best when adrenalin is flowing high? We do this analysis in three parts. The first two are concerned with teams, and the third with the exciting and heretofore not attempted quantitative analysis of the best player under pressure.

As explained in Chapter 2, the CricketX model has, as its essential feature, a computation of pre-match probabilities of the two teams winning. These probabilities are derived from batting, bowling, and overall team strengths and done so before the start of a match. In this chapter, we will also introduce CricketX's ability to make 'live' probability forecasts based on the score at the end of each and every over.

Upsets

The first stress universe we examine is that of upsets—when a weaker team with a very low pre-match likelihood of victory wins the match. An upset must have involved considerable amount of mental stress, both for the team that lost a match it should not have, and for the team that suddenly found itself within fighting distance of an unexpected trophy—a win.

Using our pre-match probabilities as the ranking metric, we find that seven out of ten biggest upsets involve Bangladesh/ Zimbabwe beating one of the major teams—an expected finding by definition and consequently not very interesting.

Excluding these two, the biggest upset (according to CricketX) has been pulled off by none other than so-called choking South Africa against the hosts Australia (pre-match probability of winning—10 per cent) in the first match of a five-match series on 16 January 2009. South Africa went on to win the series 4-1.

Interesting, but not terribly exciting. Where do we look for the most memorable upsets? Ah, the World Cups! Here too, we find Bangladesh, Zimbabwe and Kenya making up most of the top ten list—obvious. We need to dig deeper—the World Cup Knockouts (Quarter-finals, Semi-finals and the Finals) to find our Davids felling Goliaths. There have been thirty-eight World Cup knockout matches in the ten World Cups held so far. Ten of them (26 per cent) have been won by the underdogs, however slight. And only four where the winning team had odds of 40–60 or worse—two of them being World Cup Finals. Remember, by the time a team reaches the Finals, they are no longer as much of an underdog as they were at the start of the tournament.

Table 8.1 lists all the ten World Cup knockout matches that were upsets according to CricketX, ranked by the likelihood of the result, least likely first.

Amongst the most exciting upsets—the India–West Indies World Cup Final, 25 June 1983. Batting first, the Indians put up a paltry total of 183 runs against the mighty West Indies (the greatest team of the 1970s/1980s and second only to the Australian side of the 2000s in ODI history, by a whisker). In the Semi-final match, Pakistan had scored a near-identical 184 against Lloyd's team; West Indies finished off that match with eight wickets to spare.

Table 8.1 Upsets in World Cup Knockouts

S No.	Year	Knockout	Winning Team	Against	Probability %	1st Inn	2nd Inn
1	2011	Quarter-final	NZ	SA	29	NZ (221)	SA (172)
2	1987	Semi-final	AUS	PAK	29	AUS (267)	PAK (249)
3	1987	Final	AUS	ENG	36	AUS (253)	ENG (246)
4	1983	Final	IND	WI	40	IND (183)	WI (140)
5	1992	Semi-final	PAK	NZ	43	NZ (262)	PAK (264)
6	1992	Final	PAK	ENG	44	PAK (249)	ENG (227)
7	1975	Semi-final	AUS	ENG	45	ENG (93)	AUS (94)
8	1983	Semi-final	IND	ENG	45	ENG (213)	IND (217)
9	2007	Semi-final	SL	NZ	46	SL (289)	NZ (208)
10	1996	Semi-final	AUS	WI	47	AUS (207)	WI (202)

Source: CricketX database

Note: The matches are ranked by the pre-match probability of result, lowest first.

All of us assumed that India's low probability ride was over. Indians were celebrating anyway, because after all, they were playing in the Final. No shame in losing to the mighty West Indies—the Indian government had already announced a reward for all players irrespective of the outcome. Then, the upset began to happen. Greenidge shouldered a ball by medium pacer Sandhu—West Indies 5 for 1. Haynes went when the score was 50, but the West Indies still had Richards, Lloyd, Gomes, Bacchus, the talented wicketkeeper batsman Dujon, and a bowler who could bat, Marshall. Richards scored a fast

33 off 28 balls, but an athletic running backwards catch by Kapil sent him back to the pavilion. Shortly afterwards, Gomes was caught by Gavaskar off Madan Lal for just 5 runs. West Indies 66 for 4. Then, many Indians started to dream—and they dreamt all the way to a World Cup victory. Madan Lal and Mohinder Amarnath somehow wobbled the ball around, and took three wickets each to dismiss a disbelieving West Indies for 140. One of the great upsets as the West Indies chances of winning plummeted to zero from a lofty perch of 90 per cent at the end of India's first innings.

Comebacks—When All Was Lost

Their fate was all but sealed but they had other plans. Sports are a celebration of the unyielding human spirit and nothing embodies that more than an inspired comeback. It shines like 'a good deed in a naughty world'. Indian Test cricket has claim to one of the most valiant examples. In February 2001, a strong Australian side came to play a five-Test match series in India. They won the first Test easily by ten wickets; had India scored 47 runs less, it would have lost by an innings. A few days later, the venue shifted to Eden Gardens, Calcutta. Australia amassed 445 runs, with Steve Waugh scoring 110 and Mathew Hayden 97. In reply, India scored only 171, with VVS Laxman as the top scorer at 59. Australia, with a lead of 374, enforced the follow on. Who would not?

In the second innings, India were 3 down for 115 with Tendulkar back in the pavilion after scoring only 10. India lost Ganguly when the score was 232—India still behind Australia's first innings score by 42 runs and only six wickets left, their two best batsmen cooling their heels in the air-conditioned comfort of the dressing room. Then history started to happen—a 376 run partnership between Laxman and Dravid, India 608 for 5, and 657 all out. Australia collapsed for only 212—short of the target by 171 runs. This match is the paragon of comebacks—just coincidentally, it may have been responsible for Australia, and Test cricket, refraining from enforcing a follow on forever.

'That was the brightest day in Laxman's career. That innings had a big impact on Indian cricket. It had given us a huge sense of relief and made us have belief in ourselves that we're not behind... Since then, we never looked back as Indian cricket kept improving.'

~Former India captain Sourav Ganguly on VVS Laxman's 281 in the 2001 Kolkata Test against Australia

Is it possible to identify such gems in one-day cricket? One can recall some from memory, but which were they most impossible to pull off? Using CricketX as our detector, can we unearth the most defying moments of ODI cricket history? This is not something that can be accomplished by merely the pre-match probabilities. We need a gauge for what transpired through the match.

CricketX Live—Over-by-over Forecasts

Essentially, at each stage of a one-day match, CricketX Live projects the expected innings score of the team batting. In the first innings, this projected score is compared with

CricketX's expectations of what the second team can chase and a probability of result is derived. Batting, bowling and team indices form the basis of all such projections and comparisons. In the second innings, the projected score is compared with the actual target to deduce the probabilities.

All this is fine in theory, but does it work in practice?

The following graph documents the accuracy of the CricketX Live model in the second innings by number of overs completed (first innings is not very interesting—like watching paint dry, since matches really start taking shape in the second innings). It starts at 71 per cent and reaches an impressive 80 per cent at the end of the first ten overs. Thereafter, it slowly but steadily increases reaching 89 per cent at the end of the forty-fifth over. One way to interpret this statistic is that at the end of the forty-fifth over, about 10 per cent of the matches can still go either way. There is another interesting observation—there is a gain of 10 percentage point in predictability in the first ten overs and a similar 13 percentage points gain in the last ten overs. In contrast, in the middle thirty overs, the needle just moves by 7 percentage points, from 80 to 87, implying nothing too decisive happens in this zone.

Chaudhari Chase Checker (CCC)

Formulated by Itu Chaudhari, one of the early contributors to CricketX, the CCC can be used to predict whether the chasing team will successfully reach the target or not by *just* looking at wickets remaining and the Required Run Rate per Over.

<u>After 30 Overs</u>

Successful Chase if Wickets Remaining
        > Required Run Rate per Over

<u>Before 30 Overs</u>

Successful Chase if (8 − Wickets Fallen)
        > Required Run Rate per Over

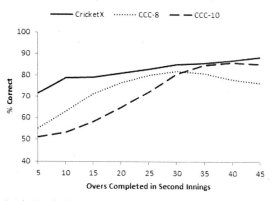

Predicting a Successful Chase using CCC

Source: CricketX database

Figure 8.1: Accuracy of CricketX Live in Second Innings

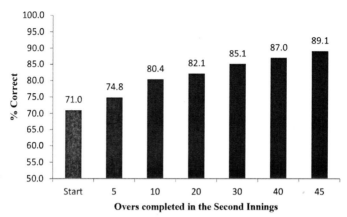

Source: CricketX database

As an aside, this live score (and probability) forecasting model was posted on the web during the 1999 World Cup and was quite a hit.

Defining a Comeback

Now, equipped with CricketX Live's dynamic intra-match forecasts, we are ready to explore the annals of ODI cricket history for acts of courage. Well begun is half done, it is said. In research, well defined is pretty much all done.

Here is our well-crafted definition of a comeback—in English. During the second innings, the likelihood of a win should dip very low and stay there for a long time, before the eventual seemingly impossible win happens. And, now the same in stat-speak—sometime in the second innings, the dynamic probability of a win averages less than 10 per cent for a consecutive ten-over stretch. In other words, when this occurs, all, including the mothers of the players struggling out there, have agreed that the match is lost. *That* is when you have a comeback.

Also, we only consider matches where the team that staged the comeback had started the match at a roughly even or better footing, i.e. 40–60 or better. This is done to remove any overlap between a comeback and an upset.

The hard work (definition) done—time for the results. As Table 8.2 shows, the greatest comeback ever was scripted by Sri Lanka at Melbourne in the first ODI of an away series against Australia in 2010. Cricinfo reports, 'The visitors seemed destined for a humiliating loss when they crashed to 8 for 107 chasing 240, but Mathews and Malinga kept fighting, spurred on by noisy support from a crowd dominated by Sri Lankan fans. They compiled the highest ninth-wicket partnership in ODI history, beating a 27-year-old record set by Kapil Dev and Syed Kirmani at the 1983 World Cup, and the 132-run stand left Australia's confidence in tatters. Malinga belted his way to his first one-day half-century and Mathews played the guiding hand with a wonderful unbeaten 77 as the pair raced towards their target with plenty of time to spare.'

In the World Cup knockouts, the greatest comeback remains the tied semi-final match between Australia and South Africa in the 1999 World Cup with Lance Klusener as its tragic hero (see Box 8.1).

Box 8.1: The 1999 World Cup Semi-final, Australia v South Africa

Australia, having been put to bat, set a target of 214 for South Africa to chase in 50 overs. Klusener came in to bat when South Africa were 175–6 in 44.5 overs, and by virtue of his big-hitting (along with support from other batsmen), South Africa entered the final over at 205/9, needing nine runs to win in with only one wicket remaining. Klusener scored consecutive fours in the first two balls of the over (bowled by Damien Fleming), levelling the scores and leaving South Africa with only 1 run to win in 4 balls with Klusener on strike. The third ball was a dot, and the fourth saw Klusener mis-hit his shot to mid-wicket fielder Mark Waugh. Klusener went for the run, although chances of a run-out were high and two balls were still remaining... [In the end] Donald was run-out by some distance, thus ending the match with the scores level. However, a tie meant that Australia progressed to the final since they had beaten South Africa in the group stages of the tournament.

Source: Wikipedia

Table 8.2: CricketX's Believe It or Not: Greatest Second Innings Comebacks

S No.	Date	Teams	1st Inn	Low point	Result	Notable Performances
1	3 Nov 2010	AUS v SL	AUS (239)	SL 8-107, 25.2 over	Sri Lanka won by 1 wicket (with 34 balls remaining)	Mathews 77*(84), Malinga 50(48)
2	29 Jan 2002	NZ v AUS	NZ (245)	AUS 6-82, 21.3 over	Australia won by 2 wickets (with 3 balls remaining)	Bevan 102*(95), Warne 29(54), Lee 27(29)
3	25 Jan 2014	NZ v IND	NZ (314)	IND 6-184, 35.4 over	Match tied	Ashwin 65(46), Jadeja 66*(45)
4	2 Jul 2005	AUS v ENG	AUS (196)	ENG 5-33, 9.2 over	Match tied	Collingwood 53(116), Jones 71(100)
5	12 Mar 2006	AUS v SA	AUS (434)	SA 1-3, 1.2 over	South Africa won by 1 wicket (with 1 ball remaining)	Gibbs 175(111), Smith 90(55)

Source: CricketX database

*implies the batsman is not out.

Note: In Notable Performances, the batsman's name is followed by the number of runs scored with the number of balls in brackets.

Choking

In the last chapter on captaincy, we looked at the performance of teams with respect to pre-match expectations. South Africa were found to be the best performers with an Extra Win percentage of 5. But this does not tell you how well they did in the death overs. Given their reputation and all the (few) instances that we can vividly recall, South Africa must surely have been withering away in the last ten overs, right? Wrong!

Using CricketX Live's dynamic forecasts, we take a team's expected probability of winning at the start of the last ten overs of the second innings and compare it to the final outcome. We do this for all second innings as well as based on whether they were underdogs (probability < 50%) or favourites (probability > 50%). Table 8.3 lists the teams in the order of their total outperformance, best first. South Africa are the coolest customers in the death overs, more so when an underdog. Moody Pakistan are second and it is England who turn out to be the real chokers of ODI cricket.

Table 8.3: Meet the Chokers

Team	Last 10 Overs Outperformance When		
	Underdog (<50%)	Favourite (>50%)	Total
SA	5.1	1.0	2.8
PAK	2.4	1.3	1.9
IND	1.7	0.4	1.1
AUS	2.5	-1.2	0.2
NZ	1.5	-2.6	-0.3
SL	-2.1	1.1	-0.7
WI	-0.5	-4.4	-2.6
ENG	-0.5	-6.6	-3.2

Source: CricketX database
Notes: 1. Only 2nd innings is considered.
2. Outperformance = Actual Win % − Expected Win %.
3. Expected Win % is the predicted probability of winning at the start of the last ten overs.
4. Teams are ordered by their outperformance, best first.

Stress

The original objective of this chapter was to identify the batsmen who play best under tension. This is a very different ranking from the one outlined earlier for batsmen; those rankings included all the matches played. It is very likely, and we will soon see the results, that the batsmen who rank the best and the greatest need not rank as the best players under tension. That does not detract from their greatness; however, it is of considerable interest to identify the best batsmen for a crisis. And why only batsmen? Because as of now, we do not possess the data required for a corresponding calculation to be made for the bowlers.

How is stress for a batsman defined? As discussed earlier, using CricketX Live we have, at the end of each over and each fall of wicket, a dynamic probability of the expected result of the match. For each batsman, we thus know, the likelihood of his team winning when he was on crease, and how he changed it. For our stress rankings, we now just need to pick which innings of his qualify as being under stress. First, as in the case of comebacks, only the second innings appearances are considered because that is where the match starts getting decided and real stress is felt. Second, only that part of his innings is counted where he was batting with a probability of win being less than 55 per cent, i.e. when the probability of winning goes below 55 per cent at the fall of a wicket, the stress clock starts ticking. The clock stops when the batsman gets out or when the team is back in the comfort zone at the next fall of wicket, if any. We use fall of wickets as our reference point instead of individual overs to avoid frequent starting and stopping of the clock. The batsman's *individual* contribution to the change in the likelihood of his team winning, for the duration of the clock, is recorded. The average of his contributions in these stress situations is the stress index for the batsman.

We have the list, we have the list. This is the list where middle order batsmen should find their due as finishers of the game and indeed, they do. The best stress batsman in the world—Lance Klusener of South Africa, with the young Virat Kohli of India, and its likely future captain, at number two. Any surprises in the list—yes, Hansie Cronje (also ranked as the greatest captain earlier) at number six.

Let us walk through Table 8.4 so that our process and the results are clear. Of the fifty-five second innings that Klusener played, thirty-two were under stress conditions. In these thirty-two innings, Klusener's average score was 51.6 and his average strike rate, 85.9 per cent. Per inning, on average, he increased the probability of South Africa winning the match by 15.6 per cent. There is a nice interpretation to this probability contribution, similar to the one we had for captains. An average of 15.6 per cent points improvement implies that in one hundred matches, South Africa won sixteen (15.6) more matches because of Klusener.

Klusener, with his baseball-style back lift, was feared as a hard-hitting batsman. He unleashed himself in the 1999 World Cup. He won four Man of the Match awards out of the nine matches South Africa played in the tournament and nearly took South Africa to the finals. He was voted Player of the Tournament.

Kohli averages 12 (11.5) Extra Wins per Hundred matches (EWH). Not surprisingly, he also holds the record for most centuries in chases—eleven—and behind only Sachin Tendulkar. None other than Vivian Richards, the best as well the greatest batsman in ODI cricket, stated that Kohli reminds him of himself!

Going further down the list we have several usual suspects—Dhoni at No. 8 (7.7 EWH) and AB de Villiers at No. 10 (7.5 EWH), Bevan, the great finisher, makes an appearance at No. 13 (7 EWH) and Raina at No. 17 (6 EWH).

Table 8.4: Best Batsmen Under Stress

| Rank | Batsman | Team | Second Innings Played | | Stress Innings Only | | | |
			Total	Under Stress	Runs	SR	Avg	Extra Wins Per 100 Matches
1	L Klusener	SA	55	32	1032	85.9	51.6	15.6
2	V Kohli	IND	70	36	2164	93.1	74.6	11.5
3	ME Trescothick	ENG	47	20	811	80.2	54.1	9.4
4	AJ Lamb	ENG	56	29	941	71.2	40.9	8.8
5	AC Gilchrist	AUS	110	21	842	95.8	49.5	8.5
6	WJ Cronje	SA	72	35	1319	74.7	50.7	8.4
7	EJG Morgan	ENG	41	25	849	82.7	38.6	8.4
8	MS. Dhoni	IND	98	67	2269	79.3	46.3	7.7
9	NLTC Perera	SL	23	20	344	110.3	21.5	7.5
10	AB de Villiers	SA	69	28	1404	87	61.0	7.5
Special Mentions:								
13	MG Bevan	AUS	74	47	1555	76.5	53.6	7.0
17	SK Raina	IND	81	48	1457	94.5	37.4	6.0

Source: CricketX database

9

WORLD CUP 2015—CRICKETX'S MINORITY REPORT

A forecaster must do two things to stay in business. First, she should forecast often. Second, she should always remind people when she is right.

~Anonymous

Shut up and take my money.

~Philip J. Fry, animated sitcom *Futurama*

The eleventh cricket World Cup is scheduled to start in mid-February 2015 in Australia-New Zealand. Who will win? Most will give an opinion, while some will beg off saying that it is foolhardy to predict the outcome.

No matter how detached, or academic one might be ('I am just interested in the analysis of cricket data'), one cannot escape the reality of the forecast guillotine. If a model cannot forecast, how do we know if it is any good or of any use? But forecasts can and do go wrong, and can damage the 'reputation' of the forecaster.

In popular media, the TV news anchors, and most guest experts, have made it a habit to repeat after every few sentences,

'Having said that'. This is just code for 'I want to hedge what I am saying in the event that I am wrong' and is one of the reasons why they tend to overestimate their accuracy, even in hindsight.

Largely, the fault lies with us, the audience. We judge analysts and their models, based on their one big hit or one big miss when we should be judging them based on their long-term record. Bad behaviour on the part of the audience begets bad behaviour from the experts. When one big forecast can make or break their careers, they always want to hedge, dithering to commit, and thus depressing the overall utility of their analysis.

Throughout this book, we have rebelled against this line of thinking, and we are not about to succumb now. So, while we know we will not always be correct (we haven't been in the past, why should we be in the future?), we will go ahead and take sides. But first a look at our track record.

Box 9.1: CricketX Was Live during World Cup 2011
If you thought CricketX has never been tested in real-time before, we have a surprise for you. During the 2011 World Cup, we posted all of CricketX's pre-match forecasts, with predicted first innings score on a blog https://cricketx2011.wordpress.com/. Back then, we had not figured out how to correctly incorporate home team advantage in our model so the probabilities are a bit different (especially for the India v Australia Quarter-final), but even then we got five out of seven of our predictions right (approx.70 per cent) including both the Semi-finals and the big Final.

Accuracy of CricketX in World Cup Matches

In Chapter 2C, we stated that CricketX has correctly predicted 65 per cent of match outcomes across ODI history (for matches played between the major ten cricket teams). In World Cups, this accuracy has been even higher at 72 per cent. If we consider only the knockout matches across the ten World Cups—i.e. all the quarter-finals, semi-finals and finals—38 in total, CricketX got 28 of them correct, or about 74 per cent. Not bad at all. What about just the finals? Seven out of ten—again 70 per cent. The accuracy is robust across subsets of World Cup matches.

Table 9.1: CricketX Hits and Misses in World Cup Finals

Year	Final	CricketX Probabilities (Team1-Team2)	CricketX Pick	Winner	Hit/ Miss
1975	WI v AUS	61-39	WI	WI	✓
1979	WI v ENG	53-47	WI	WI	✓
1983	IND v WI	40-60	WI	IND	×
1987	AUS v ENG	36-64	ENG	AUS	×
1992	PAK v ENG	44-56	ENG	PAK	×
1996	SL v AUS	53-47	SL	SL	✓
1999	AUS v PAK	53-47	AUS	AUS	✓
2003	AUS v IND	80-20	AUS	AUS	✓
2007	AUS v SL	65-35	AUS	AUS	✓
2011	IND v SL	56-44	IND	IND	✓

Source: CricketX database

Note: CricketX Probabilities are the respective probabilities of the two teams winning before the match started.

The World Cup Finals that we got wrong were in the years 1983, 1987 and 1992 (three in a row!), implying that these were genuine upsets. How true is that? Quite so, as revealed by the quotes in Box 9.2.

Box 9.2: Quotes on World Cup Finals Upsets 1983, 1987 and 1992

1983—India

'No one, including the Indians, thought India would beat West Indies to the title.'

'India's win in the 1983 World Cup remains the biggest upset ever in international cricket.'

'The rank outsiders who had won only one match in their previous two World Cups dethroned the mightiest outfit of the day on the biggest stage.'

—ESPNcricinfo.com

1987—Australia

'These are great memories for Australian cricket—a turning point in our history. We weren't successful up to that point and were probably rank outsiders for that tournament.'

—Steve Waugh

1992—Pakistan

'Pakistan had been lucky to be in the semifinals at all: following only one victory in their first five matches, they were also fortunate to scrape a point from the washed-out match against England which appeared to be heading for a heavy English victory (Pak 74 all out, Eng 24/1): eventually they finished one point ahead of Australia with an inferior run-rate.'

—ESPNcricinfo.com

Pre-tournament Predictions

Is it possible to make a prediction for the entire series and the eventual winner, even before the tournament has started? Well, that is certainly taking things too far. In the last World Cup there were a total of 49 matches played before the winner was decided. World Cup 2015 also has the same number. It is daunting enough to predict outcomes, match by match, as they happen. Predicting a full fifty matches ahead and staking your reputation on that—the horror, the horror! Obviously, we are going to do it.

Because the pre-tournament predictions are done for the entire World Cup even before a single match is played, they can be expected to have lower accuracy than our regular real-time pre-match forecasts, which are done match by match as the World Cup progresses. Even then, the record regarding the pre-tournament forecast of the World Cup winner is 50 per cent! It is not good—it is mind-blowing. Remember we are projecting forty to fifty matches ahead and have a pool of eight major teams to choose from.

To put the record in perspective, recall that in pre-match forecasts at approximately 70 per cent accuracy, we beat a random choice between the two teams by 20 per cent. Here, a random guess between the eight major contenders would give you just 12.5 per cent accuracy—we are doing *four times* as good, beating it by a whopping 37.5 per cent! With these numbers, you can bankrupt the biggest bookies of the world. They generally peg favourites at about 25 per cent (close to twice the random accuracy). You will lose half the time, but when you win, you win *much* more than you lose when you lose. Already reaching for our chequebooks, are we? Hark. Being the thorough killjoys er...statisticians that we are, it is our humble duty to remind you that ten pre-tournament forecasts constitute too small a sample to bet the farm on. We would not if we were you. The model probably has had a good run. Do not offend the God of Small Sample Sizes.

Table 9.2 shows CricketX's record in correctly picking the winners, the two finalists, and the four semi-finalists *before* the World Cup started.

Table 9.2: Pre-tournament Record of CricketX

Format	Year	Semi-finalists		Finalists		Winners	
		Correct	Accuracy	Correct	Accuracy	Correct	Accuracy
Conventional	1975	3		2		1	
	1979	3		2		1	
	1983	3		1		0	
	1987	3	71%	0	64%	0	57%
	1992	2		1		0	
	1996	3		1		1	
	2011	3		2		1	
Super 6/8	1999	2		0		0	
	2003	1	50%	1	33%	1	33%
	2007	3		1		0	
All	1975–2011	26	65%	11	55%	5	50%

Source: CricketX database

Notes: 1. These are Pre-tournament picks by CricketX, i.e. before the World Cup started.

2. In 1992, there was just one group and the top four proceeded to the semi-finals.

CricketX had identified 65 per cent of the semi-finalists and 55 per cent of the finalists correctly *before* the tournament began. The accuracy expectedly declines as we project further ahead. Also, even at the finalists' level, the accuracy has been high enough to beat the market. But again, the same caveat of a small sample size applies.

Table 9.2 divides the ten World Cups held into two groups, identified by their formats. One is the conventional format followed in most sports, where there are qualifier groups, then the knockouts (QFs/SFs/F) and the other where there is another round robin stage before the knockouts—the Super 6/8 format. This format was used in three consecutive World Cups 1999, 2003 and 2007. Note the CricketX success ratio for the two formats. For the semi-finalists a high 71 per cent for the conventional format, and a low 50 per cent (toss of a coin) for the Super 6/8 format. This means that the results of Super 6/8 formats have not correlated as well as those of the conventional formats with the team strengths before the tournament. The Super 6/8 format probably allows for more luck or randomness than the conventional one. To be sure, it has now been discarded in favour of the conventional format—more validation for our model and the decision.

The World Cup of 2003 bears special mention. CricketX got only one SF pick correct—Australia (in fact, the winner). Wikipedia mentions:

> The tournament saw numerous upsets, with South Africa, Pakistan, West Indies and England all being eliminated at the group stage. England forfeited their match with Zimbabwe, due to the political unrest in the country,

which ultimately enabled that team to reach the Super Sixes. Kenya, a non-Test playing nation, went even further, making the semi-finals.

Seems like CricketX is parsing the cricket landscape correctly. We just need to add some natural language processing capabilities to CricketX and we can have the world's first robo-commentator. Google—are you listening?

Surprises and Disappointments

Pakistan and New Zealand have surprised the most by reaching semi-finals three more times than expected. Also, recall from the previous chapter that Pakistan is the team with the highest proclivity to stage a comeback. West Indies have disappointed the most—reached semi-finals only once after 1983—four fewer times than expected.

Three teams—Australia, New Zealand and Pakistan—have each qualified for semi-finals in six of the ten tournaments. South Africa has qualified for semi-finals in three of the six world cups that they have played. Overall, the distribution of semi-finalists in the World Cups is quite even among the eight major teams.

Australia has reached the finals all the six times it qualified for the semi-finals. South Africa has been the most disappointing in never making the finals despite being strong contenders (at least three times). New Zealand is the only other team to have never reached the finals. Will this time be different?

Table 9.3: Reaching the World Cup Semi-finals and Finals

Team	Semi-finals			Finals		
	Reached	Positive Surprise	Disappointed	Reached	Positive Surprise	Disappointed
AUS	6	2	2	6	4	1
ENG	5	1	2	3	1	1
IND	5	1	2	3	2	0
SL	4	1	0	3	0	0
NZ	6	3	1	0	0	1
PAK	6	3	1	2	2	2
SA	3	1	2	0	0	3
WI	4	1	4	3	0	1
All	39	13	14	20	9	9

Source: CricketX database

Note: In the 2003 World Cup, a surprise semi-finalist was Kenya, not shown here.

Predicting the Final Score during the First Innings

Some Rules of Thumb

$$\text{Predicted Final Score for First Innings:} = \text{Twice the Score at the End of 27 Overs}$$

If 4 or more wickets left, for

Last 20 overs	Add 80% more runs
Last 15 overs	Add 55% more runs
Last 10 overs	Add 35% more runs

If 3 or fewer wickets left,

Add 8 runs for each remaining wicket.

World Cup 2015 Predictions

Now, for what you all have been waiting, probably since the time you picked up the book. By the way, this beats even the usual pre-tournament predictions as the World Cup is almost three months later (at the time of writing this). While we will keep updating the team indices and forecasts on our website *www.criconomics.com*, forecasts presented here are based on data until the end of the Australia–South Africa series, 23 November 2014.

Table 9.4: The Line-up for World Cup 2015

Team	CxTeam	In CricketX Current Top 20		
		Batsmen	Bowlers	Total
AUS*	114 (106)	3	2	5
SA	111	5	3	8
IND	110	5	2	7
SL	105	3	3	6
NZ*	101 (93)	2	3	5
WI	101	1	3	4
ENG	98	0	2	2
PAK	94	1	2	3

Source: CricketX database

* indicates hosts for the World Cup 2015

Notes: 1. The strengths include home team advantage for Australia and New Zealand. The neutral venue values for these teams are in parentheses.

2. Data as of 23 November 2014.

Table 9.4 lists the eight major teams, their current team strengths (CxTeam) and the number of players each has in the current top twenty list of CricketX. Australia and New Zealand will be playing at home and hence will benefit from home team advantage. In general, home team advantage adds about eight points to your team strength. The neutral venue strengths for both Australia and New Zealand have been given in parentheses in the table. Note the strong correlation between the neutral venue CxTeam, a macro or top-down index, and the total number of players in top twenty—a bottom-up indicator.

Table 9.5 lists the teams and their respective probabilities of reaching Semi-finals, Finals and winning the World Cup. The overall team strength of Australia after taking home team advantage into account places it ahead of others and hence is the favourite to win the eleventh World Cup—with a 24 per cent probability. As mentioned earlier, these computations are as of 23 November 2014, i.e. at the end of the Australia–South Africa ODI series which Australia won convincingly by a 4-1 margin. If that same series had been held in South Africa, we suspect the result might very well have reversed—the power of home team advantage. We are aware that in the World Cups though, only once has the home team won—India in 2011, but we promised no 'Having said thats'.

Table 9.5: World Cup 2015 Predictions

Team	Pool	Probability of Being		
		Semi-finalist	Finalist	WC Winner
AUS	A	66	40	24
SA	B	59	34	18
IND	B	57	31	17
SL	A	52	26	12
NZ	A	47	21	9
WI	B	45	20	9
ENG	A	41	17	7
PAK	B	34	12	4

Source: CricketX Database
Note: Data as of 23 November 2014

South Africa is the second strongest contender with an 18 per cent chance of winning their maiden World Cup. The four teams favoured to enter the semi-finals, in order of likelihood, are Australia, South Africa, India and Sri Lanka. The teams with the slimmest chances are England and Pakistan. Let us see if Pakistan lives up to its reputation of springing the most number of World Cup surprises. At present, the probability of an Australia v South Africa final is the highest at 9.2 per cent and it could be the most exciting World Cup final with CricketX favouring Australia marginally by 53-47 (but see our website for updates).

Box 9.3: On Hedging

In 1952, Armon M. Sweat, Jr., a member of the Texas House of Representatives, was asked about his position on whiskey. What follows is his exact answer (taken from the Political Archives of Texas):

If you mean whiskey, the devil's brew, ... that creates misery and poverty, ... if you mean that evil drink that topples Christian men and women from the pinnacles of righteous and gracious living into the bottomless pit of degradation, shame, despair, helplessness, and hopelessness, then, my friend, I am opposed to it with every fiber of my being.

However, if by whiskey you mean the lubricant of conversation, ...the elixir of life, the liquid that is consumed when good fellows get together...if you mean that drink the sale of which pours into Texas treasuries untold millions of dollars each year, that provides tender care for our little crippled children, our blind, our deaf, our dumb, our pitifully aged and infirm, to build the finest highways, hospitals, universities, and community colleges in this nation, then my friend, I am absolutely, unequivocally in favour of it.

This is my position, and as always, I refuse to compromise on matters of principle.

10

FUTURE OF CRICKET

The measure of intelligence is the ability to change.

~Albert Einstein

All good things must come to an end. It is time to call a halt to the analysis, the writing, and the fun. A lot of new ground has been broken and much accomplished and discovered. And there are several takeaways.

The Best and the Greatest

There is a distinction between the best and the greatest. The best refers to a point in time while greatness is cumulative; it has elements of domination and longevity. The best need to conquer time before they become the greatest. Greatness has to do with longevity at the top—lonely, but majestic in its loneliness.

We have confirmation of Vivian Richards as the greatest ODI batsman; while Glenn McGrath emerged as the greatest ODI bowler, and Richard Hadlee as the greatest all-rounder. The 'best' (by career averages) list is Viv Richards, Joel Garner and Kapil Dev. Also the Steve Waugh–Ricky Ponting Australian team of the 2000s narrowly edges out the Clive Lloyd–Viv Richards mighty West Indies team of the 1970s and 1980s for the crown of the greatest ODI team in history. Hansie Cronje, the fallen star, turns out to be the greatest ODI captain.

How Does Cricket Work?

CricketX's analysis unifies the evaluation of batsmen and bowlers. Excluding extras, the runs given away by a bowler are the runs scored by a batsman—a one-for-one equivalence. The strike rate for the batsmen *is* the economy rate for the bowler. Further, the batting average is the runs scored per wicket lost (number of times the batsman got out); the bowling average is the runs given per wicket obtained (excluding run-outs)—another one-for-one equivalence.

Starting from these symmetrical indicators, CricketX converges on roughly the same relative value of each from either direction *independently*. Our invention, the MES, which combines strike rate (economy) and batting (bowling) average together with the format of the game, turns out to be a good indicator of a player's worth. Its construction is symmetrical for both batsmen and bowlers and it works equally well for both. This one-for-one equivalence and symmetry between the two halves of cricket is indeed a major result from our body of work.

Using the CricketX model, we can rank players for their batting and bowling strengths at any point in time and in a statistically rigorous way. This has huge applications in performance analysis and can inform better team selection. As a simplified example, selectors would do well to maximize their team's MES while choosing a team. A team that is being limited by its strike rate should look for a quick scorer, whereas a team that is wanting in its batting average should go for a batsman who can play for long, even if at a slow pace.

Another valuable insight from the CricketX model is that the strike rate (economy) is more important than the batting (bowling) average—about twice as much. This is radically different from considerations in Test matches, where wicket-taking for bowlers, and runs scored for batsmen, is all-important —and the only attribute that is relevant.

There is a logical trend here. In Test matches the strike rate does not matter. As one decreases the number of overs while keeping the number of wickets the same, the strike rate zooms in importance. In ODI matches, the strike rate has a weight of 60–70 per cent. In T20 where overs are even fewer it is higher than 90 per cent. In other words, one has arrived full circle in that the weight was almost nil for Test matches and is close to 100 for 20 over matches.

Our analysis also highlighted how the game has been systematically distorted in favour of the batsmen—by technology (better bats and gear), increased fielding restrictions and increasing number of flat pitches.

'[F]or all its reputation for conservatism, cricket in its history has demonstrated a remarkable capacity for innovation. What game has survived subjection to such extraordinary manipulations, having been prolonged to 10 days (in Durban 70 years ago), truncated to as few as 60 balls (in Hong Kong every year), and remained recognisable in each instance?'

~Gideon Haigh

Recommendations: Bring Back the Balance

T20—Five Wickets are Enough

For the T20s, we strongly recommend that the number of available wickets be reduced to five or six, preferably five, i.e. the innings is considered over if a team loses five wickets (instead of ten), or twenty overs, whichever comes first. As discussed above, in its present format, strike rate is all that matters. No wonder batsmen just come in and start hacking away with little regard for their wicket. Reducing the number of wickets will increase the importance of holding on to one's wicket for the batsman and of taking one for the bowler. We believe this change will markedly increase the attraction of T20 cricket. It will also have several highly beneficial cascading effects. With only five wickets to play with, selectors will stop recruiting 'batsmen who can bowl' and go shop for real bowlers, raising the quality of bowling in such matches. It will also encourage focused efforts on the part of young upcoming players to hone their talents deeply in their respective skills instead of nudging them towards becoming a jack of both trades.

ODI—Undo Fielding Restrictions

For the ODIs, one can think of two ways in which to redress the skew and reward the toilers, the forgotten tribe. First, some of the fielding restrictions should be rolled back, e.g., in 2012 the number of fielders allowed outside the 30-yard circle during non-powerplay overs was reduced from five to four. This is entirely unnecessary. Second, some guidelines must be voluntarily adopted by cricket playing countries to provide a healthy variation in the playing fields.

In the old politically incorrect days, one would have said that the batsmen always got the pretty women, as well as all the endorsements. All we are saying is—give the bowler a chance.

Three-day Tests

The reason ODI cricket was invented, and for that matter T20, is that the traditional gentle-person's game takes too long. It is not a coincidence—indeed, it is a calculated design—that the time duration of T20 cricket is three hours, a duration common to most spectator team sports—football, American football, baseball, basketball, etc. Even in individual sports, a good tennis match lasts three hours! Three hours seems to be the spectator-maximizing time that different countries, and different sports, have converged on for sports entertainment.

But for those of us who have been brought up on Tests, T20 cricket, while enjoyable, is just not the same as the original. Can anything be done to make the crowds come back to Test cricket? Yes. A very simple modification to Test cricket rules can add significantly to the enjoyment of a Test match while keeping its essence intact—and drastically reducing its duration. The only rule that needs changing is the requirement that only nintey overs be bowled during a day. This should be increased to 110 overs a day and a Test should be played for only three days.

This rule change will alter the demand for spin bowlers as the team captains will have to rush through an extra twenty overs a day. But wouldn't reducing matches to three days bring

T20 Recommendation

The number of wickets should be reduced to five or six, instead of ten. This increases the importance of bowlers and restores a much-needed balance between bat and ball. More competition, greater intensity, and more enjoyment.

in a lot of draws something that neither the players, nor the spectators, can be too happy about? Not really, because result matches in Test history have averaged 332 overs, and drawn matches average 377 (both figures exclude the timeless matches in Australia between 1883 and 1937). For the period since 1 January 2000, result matches average 319 overs and account for three-fourths of all Tests. This result percentage is by far the highest for any period, and is indicative of the demand (by spectators) for results.

Between 1883 and 1937, a strange natural experiment occurred in Test cricket. During this time period, most countries had three-day Test matches—except Australia, where all Test matches were of a timeless duration. Yes, timeless, i.e. they were played until a result was obtained—there were no draws. Outside of Australia, both result and drawn matches lasted for an average of 301 overs; within Australia, they lasted for an average of 386 six-ball overs. Space fills a vacuum, and Test matches fill the time allotted to them. No reason why exciting, crowd-pulling three-day Test matches with 110 overs a day cannot become an immediate reality.

Overs in Test Cricket

Since 1980, all Test matches have averaged 332 overs. An average of 319 overs for result matches, and an average of 356 for drawn matches. Since 2000, 75 per cent of all matches have ended with a result. The time for three-day Test matches, with 110 overs a day, is now.

Overs in Test Matches

| Period | Overs in | | % Matches with Result |
	Result	Drawn	
Before 1939	295	322	60.0
1944–1979	371	411	58.5
1980–1999	324	349	59.8
2000–2014	319	366	75.1
Average	332	377	64.3

Source: CricketX database
Note: In Australia, timeless matches were held between 1883 and 1937. These have been excluded in the above table.

APPENDIX A

CricketX—History and Evolution

In the mid-1980s, there was no internet and therefore no cricket sites. Sports statistics were not even in their infancy then, but two gentlemen in two continents—Bill Frindall in England and Bill James in the US—were beginning to conceive the future. In 1979, Bill Frindall published the first compilation of cricket scorecards and in 1984 followed it up with *The Wisden Book of Test Cricket, 1877–1984*. This compilation was both the inspiration and the data source behind Surjit Bhalla's *Between the Wickets: The Who and Why of the Best in Cricket*. This first ever *computerization* of Test scorecards was accomplished in 1987, with considerable help from two programmers, K. Seetharaman and Vikesh Sethi. This was followed up by the first-ever digitization of one-day cricket scorecards in 1988. This was accomplished because Bill Frindall had in 1985 published *The Wisden Book of One-Day International Cricket, 1981–1985*.

Surjit is not only a cricket fanatic but also a sports numbers nut. 'Forced' to be without cricket as a student in the US, he fell in love with American football. In 1991, Surjit along with two close friends, Homi Kharas and Robert Lawrence, dreamed up, and invested, in what might well have been the first outsourcing job ever—they commissioned Vikesh Sethi (unfortunately he passed away in April 2014) to computerize the national, and American football league data since the 1960s. While the outsourcing was successful, the project fell apart because the football analysis team got dispersed from one location (Washington, DC) into three different locations in the US. (However, the team is still keen to pursue analysis if a sponsor can be found.)

The Birth of CricketX (database and website!)

The story begins in 1996, around the time of the sixth World Cup in India–Sri Lanka. Itu Chaudhuri, another schoolboy as far as cricket is concerned, and I came up with the idea of presenting cricket stats with a human face, and much more. In 1999, we had a website, *www.cricketx.com*, with a Dynamic score predictor, as its USP. This website was interactive with the viewer entering the scores (overs, runs, wickets) at each stage of the match and receiving the following answers instantly—for the first innings, an estimate of total runs to be scored and for the second innings the probability of winning. The website, with no advertising, was hugely successful and this led to the hosting of a full-fledged website in 2001. [See screenshot]

Oh yes, one minor detail. The year 1999 was the year of the dot-com boom and CricketX came close to being funded; but we know that 2000 was another year of the dot-com—this time the crash! One ventured forth nevertheless, and accompanied by two other 'schoolboys', Sandipan Deb and Shovon Choudhury, CricketX made all its computerized data (both Test and one-days) available to Cricinfo, later *espn.cricinfo*. For some time, one could visit *www.espncricinfo.com/CricketX*, and read articles, and process and interpret data on cricket statistics. So the next time you look up historical data on *www.espncricinfo.com*, you know where some of the old data is coming from!

APPENDIX B:

Top 100 Best Batsmen (Career Averages)

Rank	Batsman	Team	Conventional			Adjusted			CxBat
			SR	Avg	MES	SR	Avg	MES	
1	IVA Richards	WI	90.2	47.0	271	92.8	48.6	278	128
2	AB de Villiers	SA	96.0	51.5	288	83.5	47.8	250	121
3	MEK Hussey	AUS	87.2	48.2	262	83.4	46.5	250	120
4	Zaheer Abbas	PAK	84.8	47.6	254	82.5	46.8	248	120
5	GS Chappell	AUS	75.7	40.2	227	82.3	43.5	247	118
6	HM Amla	SA	88.3	53.2	265	78.1	48.6	234	117
7	L Klusener	SA	89.9	41.1	270	85.5	38.1	256	117
8	AC Gilchrist	AUS	96.9	35.9	287	88.8	33.5	266	116
9	A Symonds	AUS	92.4	39.8	277	85.1	36.3	255	115
10	MG Bevan	AUS	74.2	53.6	222	71.5	51.6	214	114
11	MS Dhoni	IND	89.3	52.9	268	75.9	44.2	228	113
12	DM Jones	AUS	72.6	44.6	218	74.7	44.9	224	113
13	V Kohli	IND	90.5	52.6	272	74.8	43.5	224	112
14	SR Tendulkar	IND	86.2	44.8	259	77.3	38.9	232	111
15	V Sehwag	IND	104.3	35.1	280	89.9	30.1	241	111
16	EJG Morgan	ENG	85.7	38.3	257	80.9	33.9	243	111
17	Saeed Anwar	PAK	80.7	39.2	242	77.2	37.4	232	111
18	KP Pietersen	ENG	86.6	40.7	260	75.7	38.7	227	110
19	Umar Akmal	PAK	86.9	36.9	261	81.0	32.4	243	110
20	AJ Lamb	ENG	75.5	39.3	227	74.5	39.1	224	110
21	Saleem Malik	PAK	76.4	32.9	229	78.2	34.9	235	110
22	A Flintoff	ENG	88.8	32.0	256	84.2	30.3	243	109

Rank	Batsman	Team	Conventional			Adjusted			CxBat
			SR	Avg	MES	SR	Avg	MES	
23	AD Mathews	SL	85.6	40.9	257	75.2	38.0	226	109
24	DR Martyn	AUS	77.7	40.8	233	73.7	39.5	221	109
25	ST Jayasuriya	SL	91.2	32.4	259	84.5	30.1	241	109
26	JN Rhodes	SA	80.9	35.1	243	78.3	34.1	235	109
27	PA de Silva	SL	81.1	34.9	243	77.9	34.4	234	109
28	MD Crowe	NZ	72.6	38.6	218	73.6	38.8	221	109
29	DS Lehmann	AUS	81.3	39.0	244	75.8	36.0	228	109
30	RT Ponting	AUS	80.4	42.0	241	72.6	39.9	218	109
31	ME Waugh	AUS	76.9	39.4	231	74.1	37.8	222	109
32	ME Trescothick	ENG	85.2	37.4	256	77.1	34.4	231	108
33	BC Lara	WI	79.5	40.5	239	73.4	38.6	220	108
34	N Kapil Dev	IND	95.1	23.8	190	101.8	26.2	210	108
35	ML Hayden	AUS	79.0	43.8	237	71.3	41.0	214	108
36	Javed Miandad	PAK	67.0	41.7	201	69.4	43.6	208	108
37	IJL Trott	ENG	77.1	51.3	231	67.3	46.6	202	108
38	A Ranatunga	SL	77.9	35.8	234	75.8	34.5	227	108
39	WJ Cronje	SA	76.5	38.6	229	73.4	37.1	220	108
40	Imran Khan	PAK	72.7	33.4	218	75.2	34.9	226	108
41	SR Waugh	AUS	75.9	32.9	228	76.7	33.2	230	107
42	MJ Clarke	AUS	78.6	44.9	236	69.8	40.9	210	107
43	SR Watson	AUS	89.8	40.8	269	75.6	33.9	227	107
44	Inzamam-ul-Haq	PAK	74.2	39.5	223	71.2	38.8	214	107
45	GP Thorpe	ENG	71.2	37.2	214	72.8	36.6	218	107
46	M Azharuddin	IND	74.0	36.9	222	72.6	36.4	218	107
47	SK Raina	IND	93.2	35.8	280	78.1	30.5	234	107
48	Ijaz Ahmed	PAK	80.3	32.3	241	77.5	31.1	232	107

Rank	Batsman	Team	Conventional			Adjusted			CxBat
			SR	Avg	MES	SR	Avg	MES	
49	AR Border	AUS	71.4	30.6	214	75.9	32.6	228	106
50	Yuvraj Singh	IND	87.2	36.4	262	76.0	32.1	228	106
51	JP Duminy	SA	83.5	39.2	250	73.6	34.5	221	106
52	Shakib Al Hasan	BAN	79.3	35.1	238	75.1	32.9	225	106
53	Misbah-ul-Haq	PAK	73.7	43.1	221	69.1	40.0	207	106
54	TM Dilshan	SL	85.8	37.9	257	75.9	31.8	228	106
55	CL Hooper	WI	76.6	35.3	230	73.8	33.7	222	106
56	KC Sangakkara	SL	77.5	40.0	233	71.2	36.8	213	106
57	JH Kallis	SA	72.9	44.4	219	67.5	41.4	203	106
58	CG Greenidge	WI	64.9	45.0	195	64.3	45.6	193	105
59	GA Hick	ENG	74.1	37.3	222	72.0	33.9	216	105
60	CL Cairns	NZ	84.3	29.5	236	81.6	27.8	222	104
61	Yousuf Youhana	PAK	75.1	41.7	225	68.7	37.7	206	104
62	HH Gibbs	SA	83.3	36.1	250	73.7	31.7	221	104
63	LRPL Taylor	NZ	82.4	40.1	247	71.2	34.3	214	104
64	DC Boon	AUS	65.1	37.0	195	67.2	39.0	202	104
65	Abdul Razzaq	PAK	81.3	29.7	238	77.7	28.4	227	104
66	CH Gayle	WI	84.0	37.3	252	73.7	31.3	221	104
67	AL Logie	WI	73.9	29.0	222	75.1	29.8	225	104
68	RG Twose	NZ	75.4	38.8	226	69.2	36.1	208	104
69	RG Sharma	IND	81.0	37.9	243	71.4	33.5	214	104
70	GC Smith	SA	80.8	38.0	242	70.6	34.3	212	104
71	AN Cook	ENG	77.6	37.6	233	69.7	35.4	209	104
72	HH Dippenaar	SA	67.8	42.2	203	64.4	42.2	193	104
73	NV Knight	ENG	71.5	40.4	215	66.9	38.4	201	103
74	Shahid Afridi	PAK	115.4	23.2	186	108.4	22.5	180	103
75	DI Gower	ENG	75.2	30.8	225	73.9	30.2	222	103

Rank	Batsman	Team	Conventional			Adjusted			CxBat
			SR	Avg	MES	SR	Avg	MES	
76	RR Sarwan	WI	75.7	42.7	227	67.5	37.1	203	103
77	SB Styris	NZ	79.4	32.5	238	73.4	29.9	220	103
78	RP Arnold	SL	72.6	35.3	218	69.7	33.7	209	103
79	NS Sidhu	IND	69.7	37.1	209	67.5	36.3	203	103
80	G Gambhir	IND	85.3	39.7	256	71.3	31.8	214	103
81	A Jadeja	IND	69.8	37.5	209	66.8	37.1	200	103
82	VG Kambli	IND	71.9	32.6	216	70.4	32.6	211	103
83	G Kirsten	SA	72.0	41.0	216	66.4	36.9	199	102
84	K Srikkanth	IND	71.7	29.0	215	73.0	29.2	219	102
85	BJ Haddin	AUS	81.8	31.4	245	74.1	28.0	222	102
86	DJ Cullinan	SA	70.3	33.0	211	69.5	32.4	208	102
87	GM Wood	AUS	59.6	33.6	179	64.5	38.3	193	102
88	NJ Astle	NZ	72.6	34.9	218	68.5	32.8	206	101
89	MJ Greatbatch	NZ	71.2	28.3	214	71.7	29.3	215	101
90	S Chanderpaul	WI	70.7	41.6	212	64.7	37.3	194	101
91	RA Smith	ENG	69.7	39.0	209	64.7	37.2	194	101
92	PD Collingwood	ENG	77.0	35.4	231	69.1	31.6	207	101
93	DL Haynes	WI	63.1	41.4	189	62.2	40.3	187	101
94	BB McCullum	NZ	90.6	30.1	240	80.1	25.9	207	101
95	AJ Strauss	ENG	80.9	35.6	243	69.0	31.5	207	101
96	CD McMillan	NZ	75.9	28.2	225	72.4	28.0	217	101
97	DPMD Jayawardene	SL	78.4	33.2	235	70.2	29.9	211	101
98	SM Pollock	SA	86.7	26.5	212	83.0	25.1	201	101
99	SC Ganguly	IND	73.7	41.0	221	65.2	35.1	196	100

Rank	Batsman	Team	Conventional			Adjusted			CxBat
			SR	Avg	MES	SR	Avg	MES	
100	SP Fleming	NZ	71.5	32.4	214	67.8	31.7	203	100

Notes: 1. The batsmen are ranked by their CxBat (CricketX Batting Index) based on their career averages.

2. MES (Match Equivalent Score) = Minimum (SR * 3, Avg * 8)

3. The adjusted data is adjusted for pitch and opposition bowling strength.

APPENDIX C

Top 50 Greatest Batsmen

Rank	Batsman	Team	Career	Mat	Inn	Runs	No. of Months Ranked			Dom Points	Avg CxBat At
							1	2	3		Rank 1
1	IVA Richards	WI	1975-91	187	167	6721	51	17	1	188	134
2	SR Tendulkar	IND	1989-2012	463	452	18426	20	29	25	143	123
3	AB de Villiers	SA	2005-	175	169	7210	31	16	5	130	131
4	A Symonds	AUS	1998-2009	198	161	5088	31	11	8	123	123
5	V Sehwag	IND	1999-2013	251	245	8273	25	6	10	97	127
6	A Flintoff	ENG	1999-2009	141	122	3394	21	11	0	85	126
7	ST Jayasuriya	SL	1989-2009	444	433	13430	17	10	11	82	127
8	MEK Hussey	AUS	2004-12	185	157	5442	17	10	9	80	128
9	N Kapil Dev	IND	1978-94	225	198	3783	9	23	4	77	131
10	M Azharuddin	IND	1985-2000	334	308	9378	12	14	7	71	123
11	DR Martyn	AUS	1992-2006	208	182	5346	18	5	0	64	122
12	Saleem Malik	PAK	1982-99	283	256	7170	9	13	7	60	121
13	CH Lloyd	WI	1973-85	87	69	1977	10	7	7	51	127
13	ME Waugh	AUS	1988-2002	244	236	8500	14	4	1	51	122
15	DM Jones	AUS	1984-94	164	161	6068	13	2	7	50	127

Rank	Batsman	Team	Career	Mat	Inn	Runs	No. of Months Ranked			Dom Points	Avg CxBat At Rank 1
							1	2	3		
16	A Ranatunga	SL	1982-99	269	255	7456	4	13	11	49	117
17	AC Gilchrist	AUS	1996-2008	287	279	9619	3	7	25	48	120
18	L Klusener	SA	1996-2004	171	137	3576	13	0	4	43	138
19	HM Amla	SA	2008-	103	100	4946	0	12	16	40	
20	Javed Miandad	PAK	1975-96	233	218	7381	0	16	4	36	
21	MS Dhoni	IND	2004-	250	219	8192	0	10	15	35	
22	RT Ponting	AUS	1995-2012	375	365	13704	3	8	9	34	121
23	MG Bevan	AUS	1994-2004	232	196	6912	2	6	15	33	125
23	BC Lara	WI	1990-2007	298	289	10405	5	3	12	33	123
25	PA de Silva	SL	1984-2003	308	296	9284	0	11	10	32	
26	Abdul Razzaq	PAK	1996-2011	265	228	5080	0	12	3	27	
27	GS Chappell	AUS	1971-83	74	72	2331	5	1	8	25	123
28	Saeed Anwar	PAK	1989-2003	247	244	8824	4	2	7	23	123
28	JN Rhodes	SA	1992-2003	245	220	5935	6	1	3	23	121
30	Inzamam-ul-Haq	PAK	1991-2007	378	350	11739	0	7	7	21	
31	CZ Harris	NZ	1990-2004	249	213	4379	2	6	2	20	121
31	RJ Hadlee	NZ	1973-90	115	98	1751	0	4	12	20	
31	SC Ganguly	IND	1992-2007	311	300	11363	0	6	8	20	
34	Zaheer Abbas	PAK	1974-85	62	60	2572	0	3	13	19	

Rank	Batsman	Team	Career	Mat	Inn	Runs	No. of Months Ranked			Dom Points	Avg CxBat At Rank 1
							1	2	3		
35	Yuvraj Singh	IND	2000-13	293	268	8329	1	7	0	17	119
36	SR Waugh	AUS	1986-2002	325	288	7569	0	5	3	13	
36	DJG Sammy	WI	2004-	114	96	1587	0	6	1	13	
36	KP Pietersen	ENG	2004-13	136	125	4440	1	5	0	13	126
39	VG Kambli	IND	1991-2000	104	97	2477	0	4	4	12	
39	AL Logie	WI	1981-93	158	133	2809	0	0	12	12	
41	JDP Oram	NZ	2001-12	159	116	2434	0	1	6	8	
42	RP Arnold	SL	1997-2007	180	155	3950	0	3	1	7	
43	CD McMillan	NZ	1997-2007	195	183	4707	0	2	2	6	
44	IT Botham	ENG	1976-92	116	106	2113	0	2	1	5	
44	KC Sangakkara	SL	2000-	382	360	12918	0	1	3	5	
44	MD Crowe	NZ	1982-95	143	140	4704	0	1	3	5	
47	Shakib Al Hasan	BAN	2006-	138	132	3936	1	0	1	4	106
47	SR Watson	AUS	2002-	178	157	5421	0	0	4	4	
47	ME Trescothick	ENG	2000-06	123	122	4335	0	1	2	4	
47	Yousuf Youhana	PAK	1998-2010	288	273	9720	0	1	2	4	

Notes: 1. The batsmen are ranked by their Domination Points.

2. Domination Points = (No. of Months Ranked 1) * 3 + (No. of Months Ranked 2) * 2 + (No. of Months Ranked 3) * 1

3. Each month, batsmen are ranked on their batting index CxBat computed on the basis of their last 30 innings.

4. Avg CxBat at Rank 1 is the average of the player's batting index CxBat when he was ranked 1.

APPENDIX D

Top 100 Best Bowlers (Career Averages)

Rank	Bowler	Team	Conventional			Adjusted			CxBowl
			Econ	Avg	MES	Econ	Avg	MES	
1	J Garner	WI	31.0	18.8	151	32.7	20.4	163	123
2	LL Tsotsobe	SA	47.5	25.0	200	42.4	19.8	158	120
3	SE Bond	NZ	42.9	20.9	167	41.2	20.4	163	119
4	SM Pollock	SA	36.8	24.5	184	34.8	23.5	174	116
5	AME Roberts	WI	34.1	20.4	163	35.6	22.1	177	116
6	CEL Ambrose	WI	34.8	24.1	174	34.8	25.4	174	116
7	DK Lillee	AUS	36.0	20.8	167	37.3	22.1	177	115
8	GD McGrath	AUS	38.8	22.0	176	37.2	22.3	178	115
9	MA Holding	WI	33.3	21.4	166	35.4	24.7	177	115
10	RJ Hadlee	NZ	33.4	21.6	167	36.7	25.1	184	112
11	B Lee	AUS	47.6	23.4	187	44.2	22.5	180	112
12	TM Alderman	AUS	36.6	23.4	183	37.8	23.6	189	111
13	GF Lawson	AUS	36.5	29.5	183	36.4	30.2	182	111
14	MD Marshall	WI	35.4	27.0	177	37.1	27.9	185	111
15	PS de Villiers	SA	35.8	27.7	179	36.1	32.0	181	110
16	M Ntini	SA	45.3	24.7	197	42.5	23.3	186	110
17	Saeed Ajmal	PAK	41.4	22.2	177	40.0	23.7	189	110
18	M Muralitharan	SL	39.3	23.1	185	38.2	25.3	191	110
19	DW Fleming	AUS	44.2	25.4	203	41.5	23.7	190	110
20	CJ McKay	AUS	47.8	24.4	195	43.0	23.6	188	109
21	A Nel	SA	46.3	27.7	222	43.4	23.5	188	109
22	CA Walsh	WI	38.4	30.5	192	37.5	30.4	188	109

Rank	Bowler	Team	Conventional			Adjusted			CxBowl
			Econ	Avg	MES	Econ	Avg	MES	
23	AA Donald	SA	41.5	21.8	174	42.1	24.0	192	109
24	WPUJC Vaas	SL	41.9	27.5	209	39.6	24.6	197	108
25	N Kapil Dev	IND	37.2	27.5	186	38.0	30.2	190	108
26	NW Bracken	AUS	44.2	24.4	195	40.5	24.6	196	108
27	PAJ DeFreitas	ENG	39.7	32.8	198	38.1	31.9	190	107
28	JN Gillespie	AUS	42.1	25.4	203	39.2	27.9	196	107
29	GR Larsen	NZ	37.7	35.4	188	37.3	36.9	187	107
30	SCJ Broad	ENG	52.3	28.4	227	45.4	24.5	196	106
31	Shoaib Akhtar	PAK	47.7	25.0	200	45.4	24.6	196	106
32	Wasim Akram	PAK	39.0	23.5	188	40.2	26.3	201	106
33	EJ Chatfield	NZ	35.8	25.8	179	39.3	30.2	196	106
34	Harbhajan Singh	IND	43.0	33.4	215	39.0	31.6	195	106
35	Imran Khan	PAK	39.0	26.6	195	39.9	28.4	199	106
36	PR Reiffel	AUS	39.3	29.2	196	39.9	28.3	200	106
37	RM Hogg	AUS	39.6	28.4	198	39.4	30.3	197	106
38	A Flintoff	ENG	44.0	24.4	195	40.7	26.1	203	106
39	MG Johnson	AUS	48.3	25.7	206	44.7	25.1	200	105
40	BP Patterson	WI	43.4	24.5	196	43.5	25.4	204	105
41	Mohammad Hafeez	PAK	40.6	35.0	203	39.4	33.5	197	105
42	M Morkel	SA	49.4	24.3	194	44.2	25.4	203	105
43	IT Botham	ENG	40.1	28.5	200	40.6	28.8	203	105
44	Saqlain Mushtaq	PAK	42.9	21.8	174	42.2	25.7	206	105
45	Abdul Qadir	PAK	40.6	26.2	203	41.1	27.0	205	105
46	CJ McDermott	AUS	40.4	24.7	198	41.2	26.7	206	105
47	KD Mills	NZ	47.3	26.8	215	44.5	25.5	204	105
48	IK Pathan	IND	52.7	29.7	238	46.3	25.3	203	104

Rank	Bowler	Team	Conventional			Adjusted			CxBowl
			Econ	Avg	MES	Econ	Avg	MES	
49	BAW Mendis	SL	45.9	20.8	166	44.6	25.6	205	104
50	R Ashwin	IND	49.0	32.5	245	41.3	28.0	207	104
51	DL Vettori	NZ	41.2	31.8	206	40.0	33.2	200	104
52	SK Warne	AUS	42.5	25.7	206	41.6	27.4	208	104
53	A Kumble	IND	43.1	30.9	215	40.7	31.8	204	103
54	JDP Oram	NZ	43.8	29.2	219	41.6	30.6	208	103
55	RA Harper	WI	39.8	34.3	199	40.4	35.8	202	103
56	J Srinath	IND	44.5	28.1	222	42.8	26.9	214	102
57	D Gough	ENG	44.0	26.4	211	42.8	27.2	214	102
58	Naved-ul-Hasan	PAK	55.8	29.3	234	49.1	26.0	208	102
59	DW Steyn	SA	48.3	25.7	205	43.2	26.9	215	102
60	Waqar Younis	PAK	46.9	23.8	191	48.5	26.1	209	102
61	DNT Zoysa	SL	45.3	29.8	226	45.0	26.7	213	102
62	CL Hooper	WI	43.6	36.1	218	41.3	34.0	206	102
63	IR Bishop	WI	43.3	26.5	212	43.3	26.9	215	102
64	Aaqib Javed	PAK	42.8	31.4	214	42.3	29.9	212	102
65	RA Jadeja	IND	47.9	32.3	240	41.5	33.8	208	102
66	KMDN Kulasekara	SL	47.8	34.1	239	42.6	29.9	213	101
67	WKM Benjamin	WI	41.6	30.8	208	42.4	30.9	212	101
68	N Boje	SA	45.1	35.6	226	41.4	34.9	207	101
69	JE Taylor	WI	48.8	27.3	218	45.5	26.9	216	101
70	M Dillon	WI	46.2	32.4	231	43.2	29.8	216	101
71	NLTC Perera	SL	55.5	28.0	224	47.6	26.9	215	101
72	JM Anderson	ENG	49.4	29.1	233	45.3	27.3	218	101
73	M Prabhakar	IND	42.8	28.9	214	43.2	30.7	216	100

Rank	Bowler	Team	Conventional			Adjusted			CxBowl
			Econ	Avg	MES	Econ	Avg	MES	
74	HDPK Dharmasena	SL	42.8	36.2	214	41.3	39.4	206	100
75	SP O'Donnell	AUS	42.8	28.7	214	43.6	29.4	218	100
76	C Pringle	NZ	44.5	23.9	191	45.1	27.5	220	100
77	GB Hogg	AUS	45.2	26.8	215	43.6	30.4	218	100
78	AB Agarkar	IND	50.7	27.9	223	48.3	27.2	218	100
79	CZ Harris	NZ	42.8	37.5	214	42.0	38.2	210	100
80	BKV Prasad	IND	46.7	32.3	234	43.6	31.1	218	100
81	SR Watson	AUS	49.2	30.9	246	43.6	31.4	218	100
82	Mushtaq Ahmed	PAK	42.6	33.3	213	43.6	31.7	218	100
83	HH Streak	ZIM	45.2	29.8	226	44.1	30.0	220	100
84	Z Khan	IND	49.3	29.4	235	44.7	28.1	223	99
85	DK Morrison	NZ	45.4	27.5	220	45.7	28.0	224	99
86	RJ Shastri	IND	42.2	36.0	211	42.8	37.1	214	99
87	WJ Cronje	SA	44.4	34.8	222	43.4	35.0	217	99
88	PL Taylor	AUS	41.8	28.2	209	44.1	32.4	221	99
89	GP Wickramasinghe	SL	45.3	39.6	227	43.9	33.5	220	99
90	Mudassar Nazar	PAK	42.4	30.9	212	44.4	32.3	222	98
91	SB Styris	NZ	47.5	35.3	237	44.0	34.1	220	98
92	JH Kallis	SA	48.4	31.8	242	45.1	30.4	225	98
93	R Rampaul	WI	50.8	29.2	234	49.7	27.9	223	98
94	Shakib Al Hasan	BAN	42.9	28.4	214	44.6	33.1	223	98
95	DR Tuffey	NZ	48.9	32.1	245	46.8	28.6	229	98
96	Yuvraj Singh	IND	51.0	38.2	255	44.0	36.8	220	98
97	L Klusener	SA	47.0	30.0	235	45.3	32.4	226	97
98	SL Malinga	SL	52.2	27.2	218	48.1	28.6	229	97

Rank	Bowler	Team	Conventional			Adjusted			CxBowl
			Econ	Avg	MES	Econ	Avg	MES	
99	Abdul Razzaq	PAK	47.0	31.8	235	45.6	31.8	228	97
100	Shahid Afridi	PAK	46.3	34.1	232	44.4	37.3	222	97

Notes: 1. The bowlers are ranked by their CxBowl (CricketX Bowling Index).

2. MES (Match Equivalent Score) = minimum (Econ * 5, Avg * 8)

3. The adjusted data is adjusted for pitch, opposition batting strength and quality of wickets taken.

APPENDIX E

Top 50 Greatest Bowlers

Rank	Bowler	Team	Career	Mat	Runs	Wickets	No. of Months Ranked			Dom Points	Avg CxBowl At Rank 1
							1	2	3		
1	GD McGrath	AUS	1993–2007	248	8391	381	39	36	9	198	130
2	CEL Ambrose	WI	1988–2000	175	5429	225	36	18	20	164	125
3	J Garner	WI	1977–1987	98	2752	146	30	1	7	99	144
3	M Muralitharan	SL	1993–2011	341	12326	534	17	20	8	99	130
5	SM Pollock	SA	1996–2008	297	9631	393	17	9	16	85	131
6	WPUJC Vaas	SL	1994–2008	320	11014	400	11	15	17	80	129
7	RJ Hadlee	NZ	1973–1990	112	3407	158	9	23	3	76	133
8	GF Lawson	AUS	1980–1989	79	2592	88	14	9	15	75	123
8	AA Donald	SA	1991–2003	162	5926	272	9	18	12	75	125
10	SCJ Broad	ENG	2006–	108	4767	168	5	16	10	57	123
11	Waqar Younis	PAK	1989–2003	258	9919	416	15	2	4	53	127
11	KD Mills	NZ	2001–	165	6331	236	4	20	1	53	120
13	KMDN Kulasekara	SL	2003–	157	5799	170	16	1	1	51	125
14	SE Bond	NZ	2002–2010	80	3070	147	4	9	19	49	125
15	MA Holding	WI	1976–1987	102	3034	142	12	5	0	46	124

Rank	Bowler	Team	Career	Mat	Runs	Wickets	No. of Months Ranked			Dom Points	Avg CxBowl At
							1	2	3		Rank 1
16	Saqlain Mushtaq	PAK	1995–2003	165	6275	288	6	12	3	45	127
17	Saeed Ajmal	PAK	2008–	110	4059	183	5	11	0	37	121
18	MD Marshall	WI	1980–1992	134	4233	157	4	4	13	33	123
19	M Morkel	SA	2007–	85	3591	148	0	10	12	32	
20	M Ntini	SA	1998–2009	171	6559	266	3	4	14	31	129
21	DK Lillee	AUS	1972–1983	63	2145	103	5	7	1	30	135
22	LL Tsotsobe	SA	2009–2013	60	2347	94	9	0	1	28	132
23	CA Walsh	WI	1985–2000	204	6918	227	1	10	4	27	117
24	B Lee	AUS	2000–2012	217	8877	380	2	6	5	23	130
25	NW Bracken	AUS	2001–2009	116	4240	174	7	0	1	22	133
26	Mohammad Hafeez	PAK	2003–	140	4273	122	5	1	4	21	120
27	Imran Khan	PAK	1974–1992	153	4844	182	0	6	5	17	
28	SR Watson	AUS	2002–	153	5064	164	1	3	7	16	120
28	A Nel	SA	2001–2008	76	2935	106	4	0	4	16	122
30	JM Anderson	ENG	2002–	181	7480	257	5	0	0	15	123
31	A Kumble	IND	1990–2007	265	10412	337	2	2	3	13	122
32	PS de Villiers	SA	1992–1997	82	2636	95	0	6	0	12	
33	CJ McDermott	AUS	1985–1996	138	5018	203	0	2	7	11	
34	DL Vettori	NZ	1997–	260	9030	284	0	1	8	10	

Rank	Bowler	Team	Career	Mat	Runs	Wickets	No. of Months Ranked			Dom Points	Avg CxBowl At
							1	2	3		Rank 1
34	PAJ DeFreitas	ENG	1987–1997	103	3775	115	0	4	2	10	
36	TM Alderman	AUS	1981–1991	65	2056	88	0	3	3	9	
36	Aaqib Javed	PAK	1988–1998	159	5721	182	0	2	5	9	
38	Shoaib Akhtar	PAK	1998–2011	162	6169	247	0	0	7	7	
38	PR Reiffel	AUS	1992–1999	92	3096	106	1	0	4	7	120
40	MG Johnson	AUS	2005–	141	5685	221	0	1	4	6	
40	D Gough	ENG	1994–2005	156	6209	235	0	0	6	6	
42	SK Warne	AUS	1993–2003	191	7541	293	1	1	0	5	120
42	R Rampaul	WI	2003–	86	3361	115	1	1	0	5	115
44	N Kapil Dev	IND	1978–1994	221	6945	253	0	0	4	4	
44	DW Steyn	SA	2006–	92	3720	145	1	0	1	4	116
46	JDP Oram	NZ	2001–2012	154	5047	173	0	0	3	3	
46	IT Botham	ENG	1976–1992	115	4139	145	0	0	3	3	
46	DW Fleming	AUS	1994–2001	88	3402	134	0	0	3	3	
46	Shakib Al Hasan	BAN	2006–	137	5005	176	1	0	0	3	102
46	JN Gillespie	AUS	1996–2005	96	3611	142	0	0	3	3	

Notes: 1. The bowlers are ranked by their Domination Points.
2. Domination Points = (No. of Months Ranked 1) * 3 + (No. of Months Ranked 2) * 2 + (No. of Months Ranked 3) * 1
3. Each month, bowlers are ranked on their bowling index CxBowl computed on the basis of their last 30 innings.
4. Avg CxBowl at Rank 1 is the average of the player's bowling index when he was ranked 1.

REFERENCES

Allen, David R. *Arlott On Cricket—His Writings on the Game*. London: Fontana, 1985.

Arlott, John. *100 Greatest Batsmen*. London: Queen Anne Press, 1986.

Bhalla, Surjit S. *Between the Wickets: The Who and Why of the Best in Cricket*. New Delhi: Living Media, 1987.

Bradman, Donald. *A Farewell to Cricket—An Autobiography*. London: David Higham Associates, 1950.

Bright-Holmes, John. *The Joy of Cricket—Portraits of Great Players*. London: Peerage Books, 1986.

The Wisden Book of Test Cricket, 1877–1984. London: Queen Anne Press, 1985.

The Wisden Book of Cricket Records. London: Queen Anne Press, 1986.

Limited-Overs International Cricket: The Complete Record. London: Headline Book Publishing, 1997.

Graveney, Tom, and Norman Giller. *The Ten Greatest Test Teams*. London: Sidgwick and Jackson, 1988.

Gregory, Kenneth, ed. *In Celebration of Cricket*. London: Pavilion Books, 1987.

Grove, William M., David H. Zald, Boyd S. Lebow, Beth E. Snitz, and Chad Nelson. 'Clinical versus mechanical prediction: a Meta-analysis.' *Psychological Assessment* 12, No. 1 (2000): 19-30.

Kahneman, Daniel. *Thinking, Fast and Slow*. Macmillan, 2011.

Khan, Imran. *All Round View*. London: Chatto & Windus, 1988.

James, Bill. *The Bill James Historical Baseball Abstract*. New York: Villard

Books, 1986.

James, C.L.R. *Beyond a Boundary*. London: Stanley Paul, 1963.

Lewis, Michael. *Moneyball: The Art of Winning an Unfair Game*. W.W. Norton & Company, 2004.

Manley, Michael. *A History of West Indies Cricket*. London: Andre Deutsche Ltd, 1988.

Martin-Jenkins, Christopher. *The Complete Who's Who of Test Cricketers*. London: Queen Anne Press, 1987.

Plumptre, George, ed. *Swanton E.W.: Back Page Cricket—A Century of Newspaper Coverage*. London: Queen Anne Press, 1987.

Rajadhyaksha, Niranjan. 'Why Rohit Sharma's 264 is not Really Good News for Cricket.' *Mint*, 13 November 2014.

Seidel, Michael. *Streak: Joe DiMaggio and the Summer of '41*. New York: McGraw-Hill, 1988.

Sobers, Sir Garfield, and Brian Scovell. *Sobers—Twenty Years at the Top*. London: Macmillan, 1987.

Tetlock, Philip. *Expert Political Judgment: How Good Is It? How Can We Know?* Princeton University Press, 2005.

ACKNOWLEDGMENTS

It is said writing a book is not tough, it is a nightmare. It would have certainly been so if it was not for our economist colleague Prasanthi Ramakrishnan, who tirelessly doubled up as our in-house editor, proof-reader and fact-checker. Her attention to details should make any publishing house drool. (We have already asked her about it—'I can't do this for a living' was the reply.) We are sure publishing's loss will be economics' gain. Speaking of publishing, we can't thank our editors at Rupa Publications—Ritu and Meenakshi enough, for their courage in trusting us to deliver the manuscript in less than three months. All our estimates turned out to be optimistic (note to selves: use a model next time) and there were missed deadlines but they were always encouraging and accommodating, even if nervously so.

We would also like to thank Itu Chaudhuri and Farrukh Iqbal for reading manuscripts and their criticisms and insights.

I (Surjit) have known Itu and Farrukh for the last thirty to forty years and the time spent listening to Bollywood music while watching and debating the contours and contortions of cricket—well, that is (almost) what life is all about, isn't it?

I have discussed and watched a lot of enjoyable cricket (and football, and tennis, and films and markets and..) with my son, Sahil, and have tried to incorporate some of his many suggestions on what the modern world wants to know about cricket—and read. Thanks buddy, and here is to your book on football and/or Arsenal!

My wife Ravinder and daughter Simran have been counsel-mates and editors of all my writing, and thinking, including economics, politics, cricket and films. Along with Sahil, I get by with a lot of help from the family. And I look forward to (only partly) repaying the debt with books from each. Now I have to go and watch some cricket.